THE
POST-COLONIAL
CRITIC

LITERARY CRITICISM

Gayatri Spivak, one of our best known cultural and literary theorists, addresses a vast range of political questions with both pen and voice. *The Post-Colonial Critic* brings together a selection of interviews and discussions in which she has taken part over the past five years; together they articulate some of the most compelling political and theoretical issues in contemporary criticism.

In these lively texts, students of Spivak's work will identify her unmistakable voice as she speaks to questions of representation and self-representation, the politicization of deconstruction, the situations of post-colonial critics, pedagogical responsibility, and political strategies.

Gayatri Chakravorty Spivak is Andrew W. Mellon Professor of English at the University of Pittsburgh. She is the author of *In Other Worlds*, also published by Routledge. *Sarah Harasym* is Assistant Professor of English at Trent University.

THE
POST-COLONIAL
CRITIC

Interviews, Strategies, Dialogues

GAYATRI
CHAKRAVORTY
SPIVAK

Edited by Sarah Harasym

ROUTLEDGE · NEW YORK & LONDON

Published in 1990 by

Routledge
An imprint of Routledge, Chapman and Hall, Inc.
29 West 35 Street
New York, NY 10001

Published in Great Britain by

Routledge
11 New Fetter Lane
London EC4P 4EE

Library of Congress Cataloging in Publication Data

Spivak, Gayatri Chakravorty.
  The post-colonial critic.
    1. Social history—1970–   . 2. Spivak, Gayatri
Chakravorty—Interviews. I. Harasym, Sarah, 1957–
II. Title.
HN27.S66   1989   306′.09′04   89–10470
ISBN 0–415–90169–3
ISBN 0–415–90170–7 (pbk.)

British Library Cataloguing in Publication Data

Spivak, Gayatri Chakravorty,
  The post-colonial critic : interviews, strategies and
  dialogues.
    1. Politics
  I. Title   II. Harasym, Sarah, 1957–
  320
  ISBN 0–415–90169–3
       0–415–90170–7 (pb)

Contents

Editor's Note
Sarah Harasym

Interviews, Strategies and Dialogues
Gayatri Chakravorty Spivak

Editor's Note

Gayatri Spivak is one of the most influential cultural and literary theorists writing in the United States and lecturing at various academic institutions throughout the world today. Her interventions into Marxist, feminist, deconstructive, psychoanalytic and historiographic problematics are well known and thoroughly recirculated. Yet, despite the centrality of Spivak's contributions to contemporary critical theory, there has been little sustained critical discussion of her work.

The Post-Colonial Critic is a collection of 12 interviews with Gayatri Spivak published and/or broadcast in Australia, Canada, India, the United States and Britain between 1984 and 1988. The collection brings together discussions of some of the most compelling politico-theoretical issues broached in Spivak's work and confronting political thinkers today. The questions deliberated include the problem of representation, self-representation and representing others; the politicization of deconstruction; post-colonialism and the politics of multi-culturalism; the situations of post-colonial critics; speech-act and critical theory; pedagogical responsibility; and political strategies, as well as many other timely issues.

Yet, the interviews between Gayatri Spivak and her interlocutors do not merely record objective dialogues, nor do they simply delineate politico-theoretical positions. Indeed, the idea of a "neutral dialogue," as Gayatri Spivak points out in her interview with Rashmi Bhatnagar, Lola Chatterjee, and Rajeshwari Sunder Rajan, "denies history, denies structure, denies the positioning of subjects." One must learn to read how desire for neutrality and/or desire for the Other articulates itself. One must learn to read the text—the narrative, historical and institutional structures—in which desire is written.

Spivak not only responds to questions posed by commenting upon and situating the question in relation to her work (a significant offering in itself); she, at the same time, attempts to render visible the historical and institutional structures of the representative space from which she is called to speak, be it as a spokeswoman for deconstruction, Marxism, feminism or the "Third World" point of view. By using the interview questions to come to terms with and to accentuate the problem of representation and constitution of the subject, Spivak turns her responses into lessons in critical reading. Each interview is both a lesson to be read and a lesson in reading as we learn the slow and careful labor of unlearning our privileges as our loss.

It was in order to bring together this active critical commentary together that I proposed to edit this collection. The interviews are reprinted in their original form. Only a few editorial notes have been added for clarification.

A collection of interviews is not possible without the work of many people. First and foremost Gayatri Spivak must be thanked for permitting the republication of the interviews. All of the interlocutors, journal editors and the editors at Routledge must also be thanked: Elizabeth Grosz, Geoffrey Hawthorn, John Hutnyk, Scott McQuire, Nikos Papastergiadis, Walter Adamson, Sneja Gunew, Rashmi Bhatnagar, Lola Chatterjee, Rajeshwari Sunder Rajan, Angela Ingram, Terry Threadgold, Frances Barkowski, Richard Dienst, Rosanne Kennedy, Joel Reed, Henry Schwarz, Bill Germano, Michael J. Esposito and Jayne M. Fargnoli. Although the interviews are the work of many people, the errors are entirely my own.

1

Criticism, Feminism, and The Institution

In June, 1984, Gayatri Spivak visited Australia as one of the guest speakers of the Futur*Fall Conference, a conference on Post-Modernity held in Sydney. The following interview with Elizabeth Grosz was recorded in Sydney on August 17, 1984. First published in Thesis Eleven, *No. 10/11, 1984/85.*

GROSZ   Questions of writing, textuality and discourse seem a major preoccupation in your published works. Could you outline what relations you see between problems of textuality and the field of politics, given that, for many theorists, these seem two disparate domains roughly divided along the lines of a theory/practice split?

SPIVAK   I think that this split is a symptomatic one. To define textuality in such a way that it would go in the direction of theory, with practice on the other side, is an example of how the institution and also rivalries between and among major intellectuals actually reduce the usefulness of a concept by giving it a minimal explanation. I think the notion of textuality was broached precisely to question the kind of thing that it is today seen to be—that is, the verbal text, a preoccupation with being in the library rather than being on the street. As far as I understand it, the notion of textuality should be related to the notion of the worlding of a world on a supposedly uninscribed territory. When I say this, I am thinking basically about the imperialist project which had to assume that the earth that it territorialised was in fact previously uninscribed. So then a world, on a simple level of cartography, inscribed what was presumed to be uninscribed. Now this worlding actually is also a texting, textualising, a making into art, a making into an object to be understood. From this point of view the notion of textuality within the Western European/Anglo–U.S./international context tries also to situate the emergence of language as a model from the second decade of the twentieth century to see how the location of language or semiosis as a model was in itself part of a certain kind of worlding. Textuality is tied to discourse itself in an oblique way. Classical discourse analysis is not psychological largely because it tries to get away from the problem of language production by a subject. Textuality in its own way marks the place where the production

1

of discourse or the location of language as a model escapes the person or the collectivity that engages in practice, so that even textuality itself might simply be an uneven clenching of a space of dissemination which may or may not be random. From this point of view, what a notion of textuality in general does is to see that what is defined over against 'The Text' as 'fact' or 'life' or even 'practice' is to an extent worlded in a certain way so that practice can take place. Of course, you don't think this through at the moment of practice, but a notion of generalised textuality would say that practice is, as it were, the 'blank part' of the text but it is surrounded by an interpretable text. It allows a check on the inevitable power dispersal within practice because it notices that the privileging of practice is in fact no less dangerous than the vaguardism of theory. When one says 'writing', it means this kind of structuring of the limits of the power of practice, knowing that what is beyond practice is always organizing practice.

The best model for it is something woven but beyond control. Since practice is an irreducible theoretical moment, no practice takes place without presupposing itself as an example of some more or less powerful theory. The notion of writing in this sense actually sees that moment as itself situatable. It is not the notion of writing in the narrow sense so that one looks at everything as if it is written by some sort of a subject and can be deciphered by the reading subject. I would also like to say that the fact that words like 'writing' and 'text' have a certain paleonymy— that is to say, they are charged within the institution and they can be given the minimal interpretation of being nothing but library-monger-ing—itself marks the fact that the intellectual or anti-intellectual who can choose to privilege practice and then create a practice/theory split within a sort of theory, in fact, is also capable, because he or she is produced by the institution, of giving a minimal explanation of words like writing and text and forgetting that they mark the fact that we are, as we privilege practice, produced within an institution.

GROSZ   You mention the intellectual. There has been much discussion in Marxist and leftist circles since 1968 about the role of the intellectual in political struggles. Althusser, for example, in his article 'Lenin and Philosophy' has claimed that, in general at least, intellectuals are em-broiled in ruling ideologies and act as their unwitting proponents. More recently, Foucault has suggested that the function of the intellectual is "no longer to place himself 'somewhat ahead and to the side' in order to express the truth of the collectivity; rather, it is to struggle against the forms of power that transform him into its object and instrument in the sphere of 'knowledge', 'truth', 'consciousness' and 'discourse' " ('The Intellectuals and Power', *Language, Counter-Memory, Practice*, 207–8). There seems, in other words, to be a debate between the role of the universal or the specific intellectual. What are your thoughts on this debate?

SPIVAK   I want to ask the question—the rhetorical question, really—does the intellectual, *the* intellectual, have the some role in social production in Australia as in France? It seems to me that one of the problems here is that even as the intellectual is being defined as specific, there is at work there the figure of an intellectual who seems not to be production-specific at all. The notion of the different place of the intellectual since May 1968—May 1968 does not have the same impact outside of a certain sort of Anglo-US-French context—I am not at all denigrating the importance of May 1968 within the French context. In fact as a result of reading the material that came out in France about May 1968 ten years later, I was able to see how important the event was. But, even within the US in fact there isn't something that can be called 'an intellectual'. There isn't in fact a group that can be called 'a group of intellectuals', that exercises the same sort of role or indeed power with social production. I mean a figure like Noam Chomsky, for example, seems very much an oddity. There isn't the same sort of niche for him. It is a much larger, more dispersed place which is racially, ethnically, historically, more heterogenous. There, one doesn't think about May 1968 in the same way unless it is within certain kinds of coterie groups. Having lived in the United States for some time, I would say that Berkeley 1967 makes more sense to me. Then if you think about Asia—and I notice you didn't mention that I was an Asian in your introduction; now let me say that I am one—there are intellectuals in Asia but there are no Asian intellectuals. I would stand by that rather cryptic remark. From this point of view I think the first question—the first task of intellectuals, as indeed we are—as to who asks the question about *the* intellectual and *the* specific intellectual, *the* universal intellectual, is to see that the specific intellectual is being defined in reaction to the universal intellectual who seems to have no particular nation-state provenance. Foucault himself, when he talks about the universal intellectual, speaks most directly about the fact that in France, in his own time, there was no distinction between the intellectual of the Left and the intellectual. Now this particular absence of a distinction would make very little sense if one went a little further afield. Having said this, let's look for a moment at Althusser.

I myself find safety in locating myself completely within my workplace. Althusser's notion of disciplinary practice in the essay called 'Lenin and Philosophy' says that disciplines are constructed in terms of denegation. Disciplines are histories of denegation and what in fact disciplinary practice should be redefined as by the intellectual is a savage practice—a wild practice—so that the point was to transform the denegating disciplinary practice—a person within a discipline—*une Pratique Sauvage.*

This is the specific practice of the intellectual within his institutionality, and within it the question of science and ideology must be, Althusser says that text, asked and opened repeatedly. It seems to me sometimes because of the historical constraints upon the figure of Althusser we tend to forget the moment and tend to locate ourselves on the text that is particularly named 'theoretical practice'. I would say that the tendency not to look at the margins, at what escapes the things with proper titles, is in itself caught within this definition of the intellectual.

Foucault, on the other hand, is not really looking at, though I think he is practicing, this kind of wild disciplinary practice, he is looking more insistently at the disciplinarisation of the discipline itself. There I think the strong moment was then recuperated within the construction of what Mike Davis has called the late American imperialism, that is to say, 1953 to 1978, when slowly the notion of power, the specific power that the intellectual must confront, is conflated into power as the same system. I am narrativizing a very complicated itinerary, so clearly I will be doing some injustice to Foucault, who remains a very important figure for me. But it seems to me that at that point, when this matricial concept of power as the same system begins to emerge, is at that point that the intellectual defined in this *very* situation-specific way, which is then seen as 'universal', and against that, the intellectual begins to declare and claim a sort of specificity, that's the moment when the intellectual begins to abdicate. We would say that that claim for specificity which is in reaction against a universality which is itself specific but cannot be given this specificity that it has—that claim for abdication is not a refusal, but a disavowal. We don't think that the intellectual placed in that situation is free to abdicate. I think this is why the discipleship of these great figures in fact transforms them immediately into the kind of watershed intellectual, universal intellectual, that they would like not to be. It's almost as if their desire is being given back to them and defined by the fact that the way they are taken up, the way they're defended, the way they're nervously followed, shows that the intellectual is imprisoned— the Anglo-US-Western European intellectual—is imprisoned within an institutional discourse which says what is universal is universal without noticing that it is specific too—so that its own claim to specificity is doubly displaced. It seems to me that their desire is being defined by their discipleship which is very quickly transforming them into universal intellectuals.

GROSZ   This raises the question that if the intellectual is in part defined by the position he or she occupies within an institution, what do you think the relationship between that institution and the non-institutional environment in which it is situated should be?

SPIVAK   Here in fact I say something which I have learnt from Foucault. I don't think there is a non-institutional environment. I think the institution, whichever institution you are isolating for the moment, does not exist in isolation, so that what you actually are obliged to look at is more and more framing. And from that point of view, let me add a digression here. It seems to me that if one looks at institutionalisation within the West since the 17th century without looking at the fact that those kinds of institutionalisations are being produced by something that is being perpetrated outside of the West—precisely during these years— then the story of institutionalisation, disciplinarisation of the definition of the man within the West—remains itself caught . . . within the institutionalisation of the West as West, or the West as the world—that is something that needs to be said too—I don't think there is an extra-institutional space. In a moment we might want to talk about how even paraperipheral space in terms of the Centre-Periphery definition is not outside of the institution.

GROSZ   There are institutions whose definition is such that they are supposedly defined as places of 'pure learning', and since May '68 in France, since '67 in America, and around '69 in Australia, as a result of the Vietnam War a number of academics have attempted to espouse their political commitments in places beyond the institutions in which they work. This raises possible problems. I wonder if you see any problems with this.

SPIVAK   I myself see the step beyond the institution sometimes, not always, as capable of recuperation in a way that confronting the institution is not. It seems to me that within a cultural politics—and this is a phrase I will use over and over again—within a permissible cultural politics which allows enchanted spaces to be created, sometimes alternate institutions which might define themselves as 'beyond the institution' are allowed to flourish so that the work of the production of cultural explanations within the institution can go on undisturbed. Let me take a *very* specific example relating again to my own workplace. I have found over the years that whereas the whole notion of inter-disciplinary work has been allowed to flourish so that it can slowly degenerate into pretentious internationalism, if one confronts questions like distribution requirements, curricula requirements, *within* the structure of the institution, one meets with much more solid and serious opposition. So many more vested interests are at work within a society where repressive tolerance plays a very important function that in some ways it's almost easier to give space for alternate activity. I am not dismissing them, but it seems to me that the whole de-glamourised inside of the institution defines our stepping beyond this.

As an academic myself I would say that if one begins to take a whack at shaking that structure up, one sees how much more consolidated the opposition is. I will go a step further, it seems to me that the definition of the institution as a place of pure learning is itself almost like a definition of the universal against which to become specific. I said a moment ago that when the Western European intellectual defines the universal intellectual and then says, "I am specific as opposed to that universal", what he doesn't see is that the definition of that universal is itself contaminated by a non-recognition of a specific production. In the same way if one looks at—of course the system of education is different here from the United States—if one looks at how things like fiscal policy, foreign policy, the international division of labour, the multi-national globe, the rate of interest, actually conduct the allocation of resources to institutions which take on a defining role in terms of what goes on in the institution, I think to create a straw institution which is a place of pure learning, so that we can then step beyond it, has almost the same morphology as creating a straw universal intellectual so that we can become specific.

GROSZ   While you were in Australia you gave a number of lectures on the work of Derrida that were rather controversial. How would you situate Derrida's work in the context of this debate?

SPIVAK   Perhaps by the accident of my birth and my production— being born British-Indian and then becoming a sort of participant in the de-colonisation without a particular choice in the matter and then working in the United States, floating about in Europe, Africa, Saudi Arabia, Britain, and now Australia, I think I avoided in some ways becoming someone who takes on a master discourse, and I am always amused to see that I am, as you say, perhaps best known as a translator and commentator of Derrida, because the de-constructive establishment I think finds me an uncomfortable person. So I will say to begin with that I am not particularly interested in defending Derrida as a master figure and from that point of view I find it just by accident interesting that it is not possible for me to follow Derrida in his substantive projects. Within the *enthusiastic* Foucauldianism in the United States there is a lot of that sort of following through on substantive projects. Having said this, what I like about Derrida's work is that he focuses his glance very specifically at his own situation as an intellectual who questions his own disciplinary production. He tries in his latest work to see in what way, in every specific situation where he is in fact *being* an intellectual—being interviewed, being asked to lecture, being asked to write—being asked to do all of these things which an intellectual continues to do whether he wants to or not—he sees in what way he is defined as a foreign body. This has led to some very interesting work, because it focuses not on what one's own desire is to be specific, rather than universal—non-representing, rather than a spokesperson—it focuses on the perception of the institutionalised other as you as an intellectual are asked to opine, to critique, even to grace and to perform. He notices then specific situational contracts. He will not allow us to forget the fact that the production of theory is in fact a very important practice that is worlding the world in a certain way. At the moment his project is deeply concerned with the problem that, within hegemonic practice, a method is identified with a proper name. In spite of all the efforts to dismantle the notion of watershed or universal intellectuals within the Western context, what is happening to the work done by the powerful intellectuals against that theory is in fact a transformation of that critique into the celebration of these figures as universal intellectuals. And I find it quite useful that Derrida focuses so strongly on the problems that make a method identical with a proper name, in our historical moment. I must say something else too. Where I was brought up—when I first read Derrida I didn't know who he was, I was very interested to see that he was actually dismantling the philosophical tradition from *inside* rather than from *outside*, because of course we were brought up in an education system in India where the name of the hero of that philosophical system was the universal human being, and we were taught that if we could begin to approach an internalization of that universal human being, then we would be human. When I saw that in France someone was actually trying to dismantle the tradition which had told us what would make us human, that seemed rather interesting too.

GROSZ   You have argued that "French theorists such as Derrida, Lyotard, Deleuze and the like have at one time or another been interested in reaching out to all that is not the West, because they have, in one way or another, questioned the millennially cherished excellence of Western metaphysics: the sovereignty of the subject's intention, the power of prediction and so on" ['French Feminism in an International Frame', *Yale French Studies* No. 62, 157]. In what ways do you see such French theory influencing your work on the critique of imperialism? (I ask the question partly because such examples of French theory have, at least occasionally, been labeled esoteric, elitist and self-preoccupied; in which case, it may be hard to see their relevance in tackling the questions of exploitation and oppression.) What do you think about this?

SPIVAK   Now, I am not going to talk about the critique of the French intellectual's desire to do this; I am going to focus on the other side of your question—how it relates to my own kind of work on the critique of imperialism. I think wherever I have spoken about this desire on the part of intellectuals in the West, I have seen it as commemorating and marking a repeated crisis of European consciousness—and when I use the word 'crisis' I am thinking not only of a crisis of conscience in a limited sense, but also in the broader perspective of crisis theory, the broader perspective of the theory of the management of crisis. If one reverses the direction, and here I am working within a very established deconstructive model of reversal and displacement, what does it say? That you reverse the direction of a binary opposition and you discover the violence. If one reverses the direction of this binary opposition, the Western intellectual's longing for all that is not West, our turn towards the West—the so-called non-West's turn toward the West is a *command*. That turn was not in order to fulfill some longing to consolidate a pure space for ourselves, that turn was a command. Without that turn we would not in fact have been able to make out a life for ourselves as intellectuals. One has to reverse the binary opposition, and today of course, since there is now a longing once again for the pure Other of the West, we post-colonial intellectuals are told that we are *too* Western, and what goes completely unnoticed is that our turn to the West is in response to a command, whereas the other is to an extent a desire marking the place of the management of a crisis. Now my critique of imperialism is not a principled production. I found as I was working through my own disciplinary production, the influences that I was working with, where Marxism itself must be included—I found that there was nothing else that I could do. To an extent I want to say that I am caught *within* the desire of the European consciousness to turn towards the East because that is my production. But I am also trying to lever it off—once again this is a deconstructive project if you like—to raise the lid of this desirė to turn toward what is not the West, which in my case could very easily be transformed into just wanting to be the 'true native'. I could easily construct, then, a sort of 'pure East' as a 'pure universal' or as a 'pure institution' so that I could then define myself as the Easterner, as the marginal or as specific, or as the para-institutional. But I am trying to see how much in fact I am caught within the European desire to turn towards the East; but how it has become doubly displaced. I think my present work is to show how in fact the limits of the theories of interpretation that I am working with are revealed through the encounter of what can be defined as 'non-Western material'.

GROSZ   Perhaps we could move away from the question of the intellectual *per se* to look at the role of the feminist intellectual. You have accused First World academic feminists of a double standard: of ignoring, reducing or explaining away the otherness of other women [e.g. "When we speak for ourselves [as academic feminists] we urge with conviction: the personal is the political. For the rest of the world's women, the sense of whose personal micrology is difficult (though not impossible) for us to acquire, we fall back on a colonialist theory of the most efficient information retrieval. We will not be able to speak to women out there if we depend completely on conferences and anthologies by Western-trained informants", 'Draupadi' by Mahasveta Devi, *Critical Inquiry*, Winter, 1981, 382]. How is it possible to avoid a politics of representation, speaking for or on behalf of other women, retaining their specificity, their difference, while not giving up our own?

SPIVAK   My project is the careful project of un-learning our privilege as our loss. I think it is impossible to forget that anyone who is able to speak in the interests of the privileging of practice against the privileging of theory has been enabled by a certain kind of production. To my students in the United States, I talk about the 'instant soup syndrome'—just add the euphoria of hot water and you have soup, and you don't have to question yourself as to how the power was produced; and to an extent all of us who can ask the question of specificity, all of us who can make public the question of feminist practice, in fact have been enabled by a long history to be in that position, however personally disadvantaged we might be. And from that point of view I would say just in answer to a specific question, the project is more of unlearning that privilege as a loss, and it will not come through benevolence, it has to be charted out very carefully step by step. One of the things I am doing which seems, from the outside, very complicated and intellectual indeed, is to search out psycho-biographies, regulative psycho-biographies for the constitution of the sexed subject which would be outside of psycho-analysis or counter-psychoanalysis. It seems to me that when one thinks about the question of women or women specifically as sexed subject either in terms of psychoanalysis or in terms of counter-psychoanalysis, what it leaves out is the constitution of women as sexed subject outside of the arena of psychoanalysis. This is one of the things I am trying to search out. Then you begin to see how *completely* heterogeneous the field of the woman elsewhere is, because there you have to focus on regulative psycho-biographies which are *very* situation/culture-specific indeed; and that effort is one way of using our disciplinary expertise, to see that the constitution of the sexed subject in terms of the discourse of castration was, in fact, something that came into being through the imposition of imperialism, so that the discourse of anti-psychoanalysis is in itself the working within a field which leaves out the constitution of the female subject elsewhere. That's one of my projects of unlearning my privilege, because in fact what is being done is that this kind of psychoanalytic discourse is being imposed upon the woman elsewhere. Also it seems to me what's being imposed on the woman elsewhere upon the other side of her more privileged ethnic sisters is a sort of glorification of sexual division of labour in other kinds of patriarchal/patrilinean/patri-local societies, in opposition to the kind of space we inhabit. So from this point of view I would say that the major project for me is to unlearn our privilege as our loss; however personally disadvantaged we might be, we are still able to specify the problems of female specificity, and that is the beginning. There is much more to say on this issue, but that will be the beginning of my answer.

GROSZ   In a number of published texts you have discussed 'universal' oppression of women under patriarchy in terms of the effacement of the clitoris, of women's sexual pleasure whereby clitoridectomy can be considered a metonomy of women's social and legal status. Could you elaborate on this?

SPIVAK   I was talking of course not only about clitoridectomies as such but also about symbolic clitoridectomies as marking the place of women's desire; but I should also say that the choice of universality there was a sort of strategic choice. I spoke of universality because universality was in the air on the other side in the talk of female discourse. What was happening was a universal solution was being looked for, and since I believe that one shouldn't throw away things but use them, strategically I suggested that perhaps rather than woman inhabiting the spaces of absence, perhaps here was an item which could be used as a universal signifier. I was asking myself the question . . . How can the unexamined universalising discourse of a certain sort of feminism become useful for us, since this is the hegemonic space of feminist discourse? I chose that one and tried to scrupulously work it through in terms not just of actual clitoridectomies but symbolic ones. My own interest, on the other hand, as I have just indicated, is in working out the heterogeneous production of sexed subjects. It is also, to move the question outside of subject-constitution—in terms of recognizing the international division of labour. There I think one looks not only at the construction of the urban sub-proletariat, since most specifically since 1971, after capitalism in the West became post-modern; not only at the construction of the para-peripheral woman, unorganized peasant labour among women and so on, but also such questions as tribality, aboriginality. And in fact—if I can throw in an aside, since you are an expert on Kristeva—I would say that for me the question of the abject is very closely tied to the question of being *ab*-original, rather than a reinscription of the object, it is a question of the reinscription of the subject. Now, it seems to me it is very useful if one can thi.ik of female subject-constitution as well, because one doesn't usually. The kind of discourse you get when you speak of the constitution of the urban sub-proletariat or the para-peripheral woman, or tribality, aboriginality, etc.: either a very hard, classical Marxist, fundamentalist kind of talk or a sort of celebration of the other. In terms of those psycho-biographies I am interested in looking at these women who are being shafted by post-modern capitalism. I am interested in looking at them also in terms of their subject-constitution, which would throw a challenge to being caught within psychoanalysis or counter-psychoanalysis. This is what I meant when I said in answer to your question of how my critique of imperialism relates to the French intellectual's gaze towards the other of the West—I said that I find that the limits of their theories are disclosed by an encounter with the materiality of that other of the West—that is one of the limits. So, I am fundamentally concerned with that heterogeneity, but I chose a universal discourse in that moment because I felt that rather than define myself as repudiating universality— because universalisation, finalisation, is an irreducible moment in any discourse—rather than define myself as specific rather than universal, I should see what in the universalizing discourse could be useful and then go on to see where that discourse meets its limits and its challenge within that field. I think we have to choose again strategically, not universal discourse but essentialist discourse. I think that since as a deconstructi-vist—see, I just took a label upon myself—I cannot in fact clean my hands and say, "I'm specific." In fact I must say I am an essentialist from time to time. There is, for example, the strategic choice of a genitalist essentialism in anti-sexist work today. How it relates to all of this other work I am talking about, I don't know, but my search is not a search for coherence, so that is how I would answer that question about the dis-course of the clitoris.

GROSZ   I don't know exactly how to follow up this question, but I am interested in how to *use* universalism, essentialism, etc., strategically, without necessarily making an overall commitment to these kinds of concepts.

SPIVAK   You see, you *are* committed to these concepts, whether you acknowledge it or not. I think it's absolutely on target not to be rhetori-cally committed to it, and I think it's absolutely on target to take a stand against the discourses of essentialism, universalism as it comes in terms of the universal—of classical German philosophy or the universal as the white upper-class male . . . etc. But *strategically* we cannot. Even as we talk about *feminist* practice, or privileging practice over theory, we are universalising—not only generalising but universalising. Since the mo-ment of essentialising, universalizing, saying yes to the onto-phenome-nological question, is irreducible, let us at least situate it at the moment, let us become vigilant about our own practice and use it as much as we can rather than make the totally counter-productive gesture of repudiating it.

One thing that comes out is that you jettison your own purity as a theorist. When you do this you can no longer say my theory is going to stand against anyone else's because in this sense the practice really norms the theory, because you are an essentialist from time to time. So, from that point of view the universal that one chooses in terms of the usefulness of Western high feminism is the clitoris. The universalism that one chooses in terms of anti-sexism is what the other side gives us, defining us genitally. You pick up the universal that will give you the power to fight against the other side, and what you are throwing away by doing that is your theoretical purity. Whereas the great custodians of the anti-universal are obliged therefore simply to act in the interest of a great narrative, the narrative of exploitation, while they keep themselves clean by not committing themselves to anything. In fact they are actually run by a great narrative even as they are busy protecting their theoretical purity by repudiating essentialism. This is how I would describe that situation.

GROSZ   You have just made a distinction between feminism and anti-sexism. Anti-sexism, I take it, is a negative, critical gesture towards dominant forms of patriarchy, whereas feminism seems to be much more positive. Would you like to elaborate on this?

SPIVAK   Yes. Anti-sexism is reactive in the face of where we are thrown. I am sure you wouldn't agree that notions of feminism could in fact be located in terms of sexual difference understood as genital difference. That is a total reduction of feminism, but as anti-sexism is reactive, it seems to me that there one has to produce a reverse legitimisation of sexism itself. If you just define yourself as anti-sexist you are indeed legitimising sexism. I don't care; as I said, I am not interested in being pure even as I remain an anti-essentialist. It seems to me that that kind of contamination of my own possible theoretical excellence is how situational practice norms my theory. Because if I chose to be pure in that sense, you know, displacing the question of sexual difference rather than legitimising it by acting to confront the discourse of the sexist, it seems to me that all I would gain is theoretical purity, which in itself I question in every way. So anti-sexist work is work on every level, not just the tenuring of women, but the work that goes on in battered-women's clinics, of para-legal work in the women's sections of unions—this is as much anti-sexist as the tenuring of women or structuring a conference so that there is equal representation. In the United States I think this kind of affirmative action is deeply in hock to corporate feminism. So what is one supposed to do, withdraw? And if one doesn't withdraw, this is not just a revisionary argument. This is a practical argument, since it seems to me that anti-revisionary arguments have become fetishized in the context of post-modern capitalism. So from that point of view one can't choose to be a purist as opposed to a revisionist. It seems to me that in that context one contaminates one's virtues by becoming an anti-sexist rather than a feminist in the sense of looking at subject-constitution—distinguishing between and among women and so on.

GROSZ   A feminism which didn't address the question of anti-sexism is in danger of utopianism.

SPIVAK   I think it's happening—in fact the example I gave here which is troubling me a great deal, when I was in Urbino at the conference on deconstruction just a couple of weeks ago and I stood up to speak about the foreclosing of the importance of the question of sexual difference or the law of genre in Derrida . . . the people who were most uneasy were the card-carrying female deconstructivists, because they wouldn't touch anti-sexist work because that would only prove once again that they were not being theoretically pure deconstructivists. And what was most marked was the unease—talk about civilization and its discontents. You know that in the German version of the Freud text the word is actually 'unease', rather than 'discontent', and that is what you saw: they were sitting in front and you know from your adolescent days how hard it is to keep up a nervous giggle for, like, 30 minutes. These women were just sitting and giggling because they felt the inclusion of some vulgar anti-sexist person. I wasn't being a 'vulgar anti-sexist' there because I was not talking about body-counts, I was talking about what was being foreclosed in the deconstructive establishment, but they were redefining their other, which was *vulgar* anti-sexism—the word is gynegogy—they were defining that as their other, so that they could be the pure deconstructive feminists. That was happening—the moment anti-sexism was let go.

GROSZ   This relates rather neatly to my next question. You have argued in two texts—Displacement and the Discourse of Women; in *Displacement—Derrida and After* (ed. M. Krupnick), and 'French Feminism in an International Frame', *Yale French Studies*, No. 62—that, and I quote, "I . . . find in deconstruction a 'feminization' of the practice of philosophy, and I do not regard it as just another example of the masculine use of women as instrument of self-assertion. I learn from Derrida's critique of phallocentrism—but I must then go somewhere else with it?" ('Displacement and the Discourse of Women,' 173). Where is this 'somewhere else'?

SPIVAK   It's a question that in part I have answered as I have been responding to your other questions. But let us bring the bits and pieces together, so this will be a sort of repetitive answer. But perhaps it should be said first that the product of the feminization of philosophy has changed within Derrida's own work. It didn't go in the direction of '*devenir-femme*' in Derrida. I should also point out that the critique of phallocentrism has itself changed within the context of what Derrida calls affirmative deconstruction—it is more a critique of anthropomorphism. There one can either go in the direction of saying that when a text is purged of anthropomorphism what one should look for is how the text constitutes the narrative of its own production. This is the way that dominant deconstruction is going—there *anthropos* is defined as human. But the direction in Derrida's later work is to see that *anthropos* is defined as 'man' as a sign that has no history. So Derrida then begins to worry about the history of the sign 'woman'. And he goes to the question of the establishment of philosophy or theory as the repeated refinding of the lost subject, and here with all due respect I would say that some of this symptomaticity is seen in *The History of Sexuality*, the repeated re-finding of the lost object. This is confused with the question of women so that the Derridean scene changed. But my 'somewhere else' is—I don't know quite what it is—but let me just give an account. One of my somewhere elses is this kind of anti-sexism which is against a sort of purity of the deconstructive approach. Derrida himself is very careful to distinguish woman in some genitalist description from the figure of woman, the question of woman, the law of genre, etc. There I part company. I think it is important to be an anti-sexist. My second way has been not only to see how remaining within a Freudian discourse one can identify the production of philosophy of the refinding of the lost objects but to find some place outside where the regulative psychobiographies construct women in another way. Thirdly, this business about the international division of labour does not exist within deconstructive considerations at all. Not that it exists elsewhere. One of the points that I have made repeatedly is that because the moment of the epistemic violence of imperialism in the seventeenth and eighteenth centuries is not really considered, the international division of labour today is allegorised into the situation of the 'guest workers' or the Third World people in First World arenas, which has really very little to do with the larger problem. So looking at the constitution of class structure, the new reconstitution of the class structure within and among women, even as that constitution has to be confused by the question of subject-constitution, has no place within the deconstructive arena. And the final task, which is the unlearning of one's own privilege as a loss—Derrida does it, but it is another privilege that he is dealing with. I think since one can't know where one's 'somewhere else' is because one is also caught within this place, which is, in the context of this question, Derrida's discourse—I can only give shadowy repetitive indications of what that is.

GROSZ   One final question. Your work can be considered both decon-structionist, Marxist and feminist. Given that these three fields maintain something of an awkward, if not tense, relationship, do you think some reconciliation between them is possible?

SPIVAK   In a recent interview Foucault has disclaimed his commitment to the notion of discontinuity and has suggested that it was a misreading of *Les Mots et les Choses* to define him as a philosopher of discontinuity. I *am* going to use the term here because I am really thinking of—to use a very old-fashioned grid—I am thinking of it now synchronically. I really think that, given all that I have said about strategic choices of essentialism and so on, the irreducible but impossible task is to preserve the discontinuities within the discourses of feminism, Marxism and deconstruction. I have seen already here how in questions and answers it can be effaced by the name 'Marxist' and how it can be effaced of course by the imposition of the name 'deconstructivist'. If I have learned anything it is that one must not go in the direction of a Unification Church, which is too deeply marked by the moment of the colonialist influence, creating global solutions that are coherent. On the other hand, it seems to me that one must also avoid as much as possible, in the interests of practical effectiveness, a sort of continuist definition of the differences, so that all you get is hostility. On one side you get a sort of identification of Marxism in the US Left in the sixties, or with what has been happening since the British New Left in Britain, or the party structure in France or other Euro-communist countries, and the slogan "Marxist is sexist" bears this hostility, not understanding that it is a method that is used in very different ways. On the other side you get declarations by figures as powerful as Samir Amin, not to mention figures less powerful like Paul Piccone from *Telos*, in the United States, that feminism has been the movement that has been most against the interests of social justice in our time. Of course deconstruction—we have already rehearsed some of those in your questions—is only textualist, it is only esoteric, concerned with self-aggrandizement, nihilist, etc. It seems to me that the role of the person, or persons, the collectivity, interested in using the immense resources of feminism, Marxism, the much more recent deconstructive morphology, is in the field of work to preserve the discontinuities, and I say ultimately it is an impossible task, for finalisation is itself impossible but irreducible. To preserve these discontinuities in that sort of sense, rather than either wanting to look for an elegant coherence or producing a continuist discourse which will then result in hostility. I think that is what I want to do.

GROSZ   Do you have any final remarks?

SPIVAK   In fact I've been wanting to say something all through this. I believe that many of these answers would have been impossible if my experience in Australia—and I have given 16 lectures in 2 weeks—had not almost obliged me to think through the implications of what I have been doing, and in a sense the place of Australia on the map is so problematic, the way in which it relates to and is going to relate to Asia in the coming years, the place in which it seems to construct itself in relation to Western Europe and Anglo-US. It seems to me that if, as someone of Asian provenance working in the United States with a certain *carte d'identité* in Western Europe and Britain, I think I have been really pushed to the extreme—of having to take stock and having to see exactly what it was that I was up to. So thank you.

2

The Post-modern Condition: The End of Politics?

This interview is a transcript of a discussion between Geoffrey Hawthorn, host for the 1984 Channel 4 Voices series, Knowledge in Crisis, Gayatri Spivak, Ron Aronson and John Dunn.

G HAWTHORN   Since the time of the Enlightenment, Western thought has been driven by the belief that it's possible to have a direct and unmediated knowledge of reality—the reality of nature, and the reality of our own nature. Progress meant that the application of reason, knowledge of reality, would lead to the conquest of natural and social evils and the emancipation of humanity. In Hegel's phrase, we would be more and more at home in the world.

But even its most fervent present-day protagonists, like the German philosopher Jurgen Habermas, agree that this modern project is incomplete, and this is quite a general feeling. For many of us, these are confusing times, in which older universal traditions and certainties seemed, even though recently to be quite solid and reliable, no longer offer the same security. We still seem far from being at home in the world.

And others have come to insist that it's absurd ever to believe that we could be. They argue from a variety of directions, from Wittgenstein's later philosophy, from American philosophical pragmatism, from Nietzsche, that direct knowledge of our own nature is inconceivable. We can never connect, we can certainly never know that we connect with the things that there are in the world. All that we can know is what we say about the world—our talk, our sentences, our discourse, our texts. There's nothing outside these texts, no extra texts. There's nothing prior to these texts, no pretexts, there are just more texts. Indeed this claim itself is just another text.

And a mistake in the modern project, these people argue, is not just philosophical, it's also moral and political. By this point in the 20th century, it's clear that too many heads have been broken in the name of too many theories posing as truths. Attempts to control nature and reform society by applications to one or another kind of reason have become increasingly problematic.

They've thrown up phenomena that are paradoxical, contradictory and increasingly difficult to control. The horrors of the modern world, the threat of nuclear annihilation, ecological crises, systematically applied totalitarianisms are the products of the modern project.

Its successor, the post-modern project, is, as so many others have been, pressed to its furthest point in Paris. Since 1968, a group of thinkers there, loosely dubbed "post-structuralists"—Michel Foucault, Jacques Derrida, Gilles Deleuze and others—have subjected many of the comfortable assumptions about humanity, knowledge, rationality and progress to disturbing interrogation.

But what's been distinctive about this interrogation is that instead of using science and reason to get to a clearer truth, these writers have viewed the very idea of truth with extreme suspicion, something to be dismantled, de-constructed. They've waged a war of deconstruction against all the "grands récits" with which we find our way around the world, against all the tall stories we tell ourselves. Scientific rationality, the unification of knowledge, the emancipation of humanity.

One leading post-structuralist, Jean-François Lyotard, has argued in his recent book *The Post Modern Condition* that *the* characteristic of the post-modern age is precisely the loss of credibility in the grands récits of modernity.

But are we still to think of political progress? And if we are, does that not require some commitment, some belief in rationality?

Here tonight to argue about whether post-structuralism offers an intelligible position, and if intelligible, acceptable, and if acceptable, liveable, are Gayatri Spivak, a professor of English at the University of Texas, who's translated Derrida's most famous work, and is herself a leading deconstructionist and the author of a forthcoming book on deconstruction, feminism and Marxism; John Dunn, a reader in politics at the University of Cambridge, author of a forthcoming book on the politics of socialism, and a book entitled *Western Political Thought in the Face of the Future,* in which he questions many of the political ideas by which we live; and Ronald Aronson, professor of the humanities at Wayne State University in Detroit, who in his recent book *The Dialectics of Disaster* asks what can be done in the face of the historical slaughterhouse of the 20th century.

Gayatri Spivak, could I ask you first whether the deconstructionist movement is a declaration of war, or the celebration of a victory over the grands récits?

SPIVAK I think of it myself as a radical acceptance of vulnerability. The grands récits are great narratives and the narrative has an end in view. It is a programme which tells how social justice is to be achieved. And I think the post-structuralists, if I understand them right, imagine again and again that when a narrative is constructed, something is left out. When an end is defined, other ends are rejected, and one might not know what those ends are. So I think what they are about is asking over and over again, What is it that is left out? Can we know what is left out? We must know the limits of the narratives, rather than establish the narratives as solutions for the future, for the arrival of social justice, so that to an extent they're working within an understanding of what they cannot do, rather than declaring war.

HAWTHORN   So if I understand it, then, they're not objecting to the very idea of producing narratives, they are, so to speak, dancing critically on the edge of every narrative that's produced, pointing out the silences, pointing out the unspoken, undescribed others that are implied in each of these narratives. They're not themselves concerned to put a stop to narration itself.

SPIVAK   I think if one can lump Derrida and Lyotard together in this way, I think what they are noticing is that we cannot but narrate. So it's not a question of waging war on narratives, but they're realising that the impulse to narrate is not necessarily a solution to problems in the world. So what they're interested in is looking at the limits of narration, looking at narrativity, making up stories that tell us, "This is history," or making up stories that tell us, "This is the programme to bring about social justice." They're looking at that in a certain way as symptomatic of the solution. We must work with them, but there are also problems. But the other problem also is that in a narrative, as you proceed along the narrative, the narrative takes on its own impetus as it were, so that one begins to see reality as non-narrated. One begins to say that it's not a narrative, it's the way things are.

HAWTHORN   Is there some particular narrative that the French deconstructionists and the English and American followers have in mind? Which they wish to deconstruct?

SPIVAK   Well, the field is fraught—various kinds of people deconstruct various kinds of things. But it seems to me that the narrative that they are perhaps all of them agreed upon as the object of investigation, is precisely the narrative that you were talking about to begin with, the rationalist narratives of the knowing subject, full of a certain sort of benevolence towards others, wanting to welcome those others into his own—and I use the pronoun advisedly—into his own understanding of the word, so that they too can be liberated and begin to inhabit a world that is the best of all possible worlds.

In the process, what happens is that such a world is defined, and the norm remains the benevolent originator of rationalist philosophy. To an extent that is if you like, grosso modo, the object of investigation. But the big word is also phallocentrism, so that there is a certain sort of understanding that the hero of this scenario, of this narrative, has been in fact Western man. So that is something that's also picked up. But that is the count against the grands récits, but by no means does it say that over against it is the deconstructive philosopher, who destroys the idea of post-structuralist practice, is an acknowledgment that the impulse to narrate, that the impulse to think of origins and ends, that these are theories that we all share. But it acknowledges that it is a need rather than the way to truth.

So I think it's a very slight difference, but a crucial difference.

HAWTHORN   Insofar as they wish nevertheless to secure some authority for doing even that, they have to persuade us. One of the standard ways of persuading us is to use arguments. One of the standard ways of arguing is to appeal to reason, and one of the standard ways of making a rational argument is to appeal to evidence, to point to things. But it seems that at the end of the line in the arguments that they're producing, they are pointing to an absence. And therefore I'm slightly puzzled as to how one is supposed to take their argument as an argument.

SPIVAK   It really asks for, as it were, to use a very old term, a transformation of consciousness—a changing mind set. It's in that sense, again to use an old-fashioned word, ideological project. To develop a mind set which allows one not to be nervous about the fact that what one is saying is undermined by the way one says it, radically. Not just make that apology and then business as usual, but actually to present us with that problem which is the familiar problem of every practice, and say the point is not to produce such an analysis that you will make a nice solution and everything else will be excluded, but to forge a practice which takes this into account.

HAWTHORN   I see exactly what you mean. Nevertheless, there is the difficulty that business as usual includes trying to establish claims which might be true and distinguish them from claims which might be false.

John Dunn, can I ask you what you see the implications of this view to be for truth and falsity?

DUNN   It's reasonable enough to say that any characterisation of human experience, any statement about what's going on, is necessarily selective, that it in some sense involves editing. But it isn't clear that anything very important follows from that. And I'm not sure that insofar as Western philosophy, particularly since the 17th century, has been directed at attempting to understand the ways in which human capacities for knowing work and fail to work, I'm not sure that there is anything distinctive and clear and true which Western philosophy could draw from post-structuralism myself.

SPIVAK   It is in the production of these theories that the great cultural explanations are produced that allow the entire capitalist caper to carry on on the other side of the international division of labour. So it seems to me it's very important for academic theoreticians not to deglamourise what they do in the classroom and what they do in their books and to question that particular project. So that I would say that it is in the arena of what one would call ideological production, theoretical production, that the blow is falling, is a hopeful sign.

I would also say that the post-structuralist reader would fix upon what John Dunn no doubt thought was simply a rhetorical part of a sentence. I'm not sure that anything—there is anything very important in what is being edited out. But that's precisely the point.

That uncertainty is where we would fix our glance. Let us look for a bit at what is being edited out, and then perhaps we shall be able to engage productively what is called affirmative deconstruction, with what the nature of that uncertainty is. We don't in fact—just as I said when you asked me the question about what is the solution. I said, "Let us take into account the structure of our own production" in the same way I would say, "Let us take into account the rhetorical gestures in what we say." So it is along those lines that I would agree with John Dunn, but I would have these particular kinds of questions.

HAWTHORN   Ron Aronson, I sense you are not quite at home with this view.

ARONSON   Let's come back to the question of editing out various voices from one of the grands récits. I would say that Marxism—what are referred to as one of the grands récits—edits out certain voices, certain modes of discourse, puts certain ones on the margin, puts others in the centre. Now rather than a great narrative, it seems to me it's an intellectual system which lays claim to truth, which has a structured sense of history and a structured sense of economic life, a structured sense of the fundamental social problems, a structured sense of how all of these operate unrolling in time. And chooses therefore to edit out certain voices, to include others, because of the very premise on which the whole mode of cognition is built.

Now if one wants to talk within post-modernism, of social justice, what basis do you have there within it to speak on behalf of social justice, rather than on behalf of social oppression? In Marxism it is built into the very mode of cognition and it's built into Marxism's position, allying itself with the oppressed classes. And that's a very clear—what shall we say?—epistemological and political choice that's made at the beginning. How does one make choices like that?

SPIVAK   One makes choices—once again I'm trying to speak as much as I can close to the text of the people that we are talking about—one makes choices according to the old rules. There are—again I'm quoting

Derrida—there are no rules but the old rules. But the thing is that Lyotard talking about rules, Derrida talking about rules, they see that those rules are rules, that truth is a matter of validation, and that those things are rules. They cannot be universalised, and from that point of view the discourse of Marx may say that it interests itself in social justice, but on the other hand we know that it is possible to use the very name of Marxism to produce, on occasion, in situations, exactly the opposite.

HAWTHORN What's your reaction to that? It gives Marxism, if you accept it, a much more contingent, much more provisional character. . .

ARONSON Yes, well, I think certainly most Marxists since—at the very least since Kruschev's secret speech and certainly many before— have been aware that Marxism is not an absolute truth, is not a set of rules that are to be followed in every situation, and that indeed it can and has been used as the ideology of a state, as well as the critique of ideology, which is really—I think its original radical starting point in radical energy—I think in some ways it shares with post-structuralism. The effort to—shall we say—"get behind" the finished social realities, to understand their formation, to understand their roots and creation in a process of social production which it turns out is antagonistic and oppressive.

There is, however, the Marxist insistence on universalism, which I'd like to emphasise for a moment. Not because Marxism is a universal truth as Platonism, as Christianity, but rather that within Marxism the argument is that capitalism itself and its structures become universalised throughout the world, and that Marxism is an effort to reflect those structures, reflect their operations and in so doing is trying to present its object, and inasmuch as capitalism becomes imperialism, becomes displaced in a whole variety of ways, Marxism tries to trace, follow and remain close to that object and itself therefore becomes universal truth inasmuch as these processes are universal. And only that much.

HAWTHORN John Dunn, is it your sense from this conversation about the implications of deconstructionism from Marxism that it leaves political theory more or less where it is?

DUNN Well, I don't understand myself how it can much assist political theory. Marxism has very well advertised limitations as an instrument for political understanding, and it's also of course true that although in its formal evaluative commitments it's very firmly committed to human emancipation, but it has been very dramatically abused in various political contexts, and of course is still being abused in those contexts in the 20th century. But what's important about it, I think, is its potential contribution as an instrument of political understanding, and I think its strengths and weaknesses from that point of view are something which can be assessed which certainly descend from the rationalist project of the 18th century, and can be better assessed in those terms than by deploying the apparatus of post-1960s Parisian literary criticism.

HAWTHORN   Why do you say it can be better assessed in the older way than in the new?

DUNN   Because what's important for understanding politics is the capacity to analyse in a powerfully simplifying way what really matters, what is going on, because in politics the important thing always is to judge what is at stake, what may and may not happen. And that involves thinking causally, there is no other way in which one could begin to judge about politics than by thinking causally. And I do not see that a very pronounced suspicion of what other people are saying, which is certainly an entirely appropriate attitude in facing political reality at all times and in all places—I do not see that a very pronounced suspicion about what other people are saying is in itself any contribution at all to powerful and accurate causal judgment.

SPIVAK   We can't throw away thinking causally. But if I can introduce a word that is often used within post-structuralism—it's a rhetorical term but Nietzsche used it in this way—the term "metalepsis," that one quite often substitutes an effect for a cause when one is thinking causally. That is a way of being aware that causal thinking has its own limits. One can't judge without causal thinking. But then to ground the cause that one has established for the analysis into a certainty is what the post-structuralist would question. The post-structuralist would say that generally causes are produced as effects of effects—that's an argument that's perhaps a little complicated, but we can talk about it if you're interested in it.

HAWTHORN   John, what's your reaction to that?

DUNN   Well, I think—insofar as post-structuralism is a generalised nervousness about how well one understands what is going on and certainly extends to the self-understanding of post-structuralists as well as the self-understanding of everyone else, I don't see that it could do any harm. I'm not speaking against there being people who practise it. What I am expressing scepticism about is how much help it will actually turn out to be in understanding politically what is going on and what it's a good idea to do. And I think it would be perhaps helpful to lay it on the line from that point of view against other persistent critiques, and other radically critical philosophies of practice.

I'm going back to a formula you used at the very beginning that what it is is a radical acceptance of vulnerability. That sounds very attractive, because we certainly are vulnerable, and we'd better face up to that as bravely as we can. But I think it's worth asking how much better a post-structuralist sensibility is likely to prove at picking out the precise dimensions of our vulnerability, at assessing the range of very direct threats which face us, and at directing us on how we might in practice— because it is a very practical matter—it's a very heavy world we live in— how we might set about trying to counter those threats.

SPIVAK   I don't think in terms of the large programmatic solutions we will be able to produce those kinds of things. The interests of understanding are better served by the narratives, but the narratives are limited, and the narratives as they save—also kill. And to an extent post-structuralism reminds us of that as it goes on.

DUNN   So the bottom line is that it's a generalised encouragement to stay very widely awake as you move through . . .

SPIVAK   But it doesn't apply to everyone in the same way. That's another point I wanted to make.

ARONSON   I came to the discussion worried about the nuclear threat. And worried above all about what one could call a very specific threat but one which is universal and generalisable. And thinking to myself what tools do we need in order to grasp and understand this threat, and in order to dismantle it, and after dismantling, which is not an intellectual one, but has to be a political one. I'm not sure what help the orientation you're developing can give in encountering that threat. I can turn to other systems of thought, Marxism once again, and follow particular structured ways of allowing access to at least some main dimensions of that threat.

But it seems to me that given the overwhelming and great, grand traumatic nature of what we face, we need modes of thought which are equal to those threats. And post-structuralism as you present it now seems very humble. As it presents itself when I read it, it seems, shall we say—it arrogates far more to itself, it seems to make the whole world into a text as you quoted earlier. It seems to banish any comprehension beyond the texts. That's what troubles me. What troubles me is the seeming self-exclusion of the world, the absorption of everything in the world into the world of discourse, the world of words, the world of texts, and the lack of concern for those problems of human suffering and a threat to the world that occupy most of my waking energy.

DUNN   The view that all there is is texts is an absurd view. You only have to hear it to hear that it's absurd. It certainly won't be a text if human beings exterminate themselves in the next half hour as they perfectly pragmatically now could—well, they would all be dead at the end of it, but they'd all be dead in the long run because of it. The radical insistence on textuality isn't any obvious help as Ron Aronson was saying, isn't in any obvious sense a help in thinking about any of the major practical problems that face human beings politically, economically, etc. But why is this scepticism of pseudo-authoritative discourse, of which of course there is a great deal (I've no doubt I've been exhibiting some of it)—why is that going to help us in the face of those problems? That's why I would like to understand.

SPIVAK To identify text with verbal text is also—I'm sorry that the word "text" was used by the philosophers we are talking about, but to an extent that is once again part of that vulnerability that I spoke of, there is a word that they use, a difficult word, paleonomy—that is to say, the charge which words carry on their shoulders, so perhaps it's better not to construct new words that seem clean.

Text in the way in which certainly Derrida and Lyotard understand it is not at all the verbal text. There are two ways once again perhaps of looking at this problem. When they read actual verbal objects that are political philosophy, philosophy of history or whatever, they like to show that those things are also produced in language—because there is a tendency to forget that they're produced in language. There you may say that text is understood verbally. But when they talk about there is nothing but text, etc., they are talking about a network, a weave—you can put names on it—politico-psycho-sexual-socio, you name it . . . The moment you name it, there is a network that's broader than that. And to an extent that notion that we are effects within a much larger text/tissue/weave of which the ends are not accessible to us is very different from saying that everything is language. And to an extent if we are exterminated within the next 5 minutes, it will be a textual event, because it would not come about without the history that we are speaking of at great length here. And if that is not a text, nothing is.

So from that point of view, the notion of text is one which has been domesticated into the verbal text, so that this can be understood as nothing more than another linguistic caper. But that's not what it is.

HAWTHORN Well perhaps that's a point at which we can take a break. We shall be back in a moment.

HAWTHORN Welcome back. Before the break, Ron Aronson, you were suggesting, and indeed you suggest in your book, that there are some very urgent items on the political agenda, items which require objective analysis and firm programmes for action, items therefore which seem altogether too urgent to wait upon this kind of theoretical scepticism that we've heard about in the first half of the programme.

ARONSON   I suggest that the dangers ahead of us are somehow connected with the catastrophes that have happened before—the Holocaust, Stalinism and so on. And that we do have the capacity for a reasonably objective analysis of those disasters and a reasonably objective analysis of the dangers. That we can look at what has happened closely and carefully, and try to understand and succeed in large measure at objectively understanding why, and that we can use these understandings to try to forestall the dangers that are ahead.

HAWTHORN   Can you tell us what this analysis is?

ARONSON   First of all, if you look at much of our century, in ordinary discourse we would very commonly say: This has been mad, Nazism has been mad, Stalinism has been mad, the nuclear threat is mad. But there's been a gross irrationality at the heart of the 20th century, there still is today in political practice, and it seems to me that the best way to get to that gross irrationality and understand it is through social analysis, social structural analysis of the dynamics between classes in societies. So, for example, in Nazi Germany, in the Soviet Union, we can look at social classes whose conflicts were conditioned by the fact that they did not exist at the same moment in time, you might say, were not synchronous social classes. That in some cases a social class was a class of the past, exploding against the present. In other cases, the social class might be viewed as a social class of the future, trying to drive the rest of the society into the future—the Soviet Union. And that there are particular kinds of explosions which lend themselves to the 20th century for a whole variety of reasons.

Also, in the case of the American war in Vietnam, or in the case of the nuclear threat, we can look at the displacement of social conflict onto technology, what I name in my book "overdevelopment". It's a kind of displacement which gets out of hand as if one turns to the genie to solve social problems, a genie which is out of the bottle and won't come back in—nuclear weapons. Now this analysis is—at least I offer it as something that can be debated, something that can be proven true or false, something that people might agree or disagree with. All on the terrain of objectivity.

DUNN   I wonder really at this very late stage of the 20th century, if an essentially Marxist way of thinking about what is going on could turn out to be anything like sufficient for directing us on how we ought to act to try and diminish the probability of even worse things happening, and improve the human quality of life in the societies which we inhabit, very different societies, as Gayatri pointed out earlier on, and all of them constituted by human beings in very different practical situations within themselves.

Now I'd just like to press you on one formula you used which is speaking about social classes, the class of the past and the class of the future. I take it what is politically central to Marxism is the belief that although human history before capitalism and in capitalism had to be socially oppressive to take place at all, that it no longer needs to be oppressive, and that what in Marxist terms causes it to stop being oppressive would be a political triumph of the class of the future, the proletariat. Now I must say, I think myself that that view was always a pretty incoherent and foolish view, and I don't really see how it's a seriously sustainable view in the face of the actual history of the 20th century.

SPIVAK I think class struggle is an extremely important banner under which to mobilise. I want to get this said before I say what I'm going to say.

If one looks at the way in which, for example, the United Steelworkers were used against Asian competitors during their recent strike, one sees that to universalise the working class under advanced capitalism, in the 1980s as the proletariat, is the kind of mistake that post-structuralist readers simply would not allow.

First of all, since, as I said in the first half, it is also a critique of phallocentrism, we would fix our glance on the fact that the notion of the proletariat itself is based on a certain kind of narrativisation and exclusion. No one in fact possesses nothing but the object of his or her body but a woman. In fact that is something that is completely undermined when one chooses to establish as a proletariat the man who sells his labour. To an extent that's the point where we would fix our glance.

We would also say that in terms of a feminist analysis, the notion of class struggle has suppressed a lot. Then we would say with all of the peasant movements all over the world that the idea of class struggle can sometimes be an imposition. And from that point of view we would say that since in Marx the notion of a post-revolutionary society is not articulate, especially in the later writings, that the notion in fact of a use-value society is extremely problematic, those are the moments of doubt that a post-structuralist reader finds as moments of enablement.

Since we are not looking for a perfect analysis, but we are looking for the mark of vulnerability which makes a great text not an authority generating a perfect narrative, but our own companion, as it were, so we can share our own vulnerabilities with those texts and move. It seems to me that those are the places where we would begin to question.

And there, if I can talk about the critique of the subject in Marx, it seems to me that that particular insight, that the agent of history is not the individual as constituted by society, the—what we have seen in Marxism since then is a move toward collectivity as against the individual. The critique of the subject then has been understood in that way. At worst it has become a party line, at best it has become a genuine desire to mobilise.

Whereas a post-structuralist reading would also say there is something on the other side of the individual. That is to say, not a collectivity which takes you to macrological solutions which in the end do not lead to the ends that had been prescribed, but in fact the subject has another side which is caught within the textuality of ideological or historical production.

So we look at the female subject, at the subject in the margins of the periphery, the subject where you find it really, in terms of its place, of its constitution. And we wouldn't make the mistake of thinking that a worker in a Ford Motor factory is tomorrow's proletariat. No. It exists within a certain kind of hegemonic ideological constitution which it shares with the makers of the rationalist narrative. So I would say that in terms of the individual, post-structuralism would take you, with regard to Marxist critique of the subject which comes out of Hegel, which comes out of Kant—post-structuralism would take you on the other side of the individual rather than to collectivities.

HAWTHORN   And if it did take one on the other side of the individual, what then would that imply for political thinking and political practice? What would one actually do and how would one conceive of what one was doing?

SPIVAK   Well, one would conceive of what one was doing according to the old rules. But in terms of how it would change one's practice, it would depend on not believing that the formula for the good end would come if the programme were adequately represented, because there is in fact no possibility of adequate representation of any narrative in practice.

HAWTHORN   John Dunn, the very idea of an adequate political programme is self-defeating?

Having got so far in intention, though no doubt not in achievement, as recognising the subjectivity of all the human beings there, the question of what to do I think is going to depend very heavily on what you've called the old rules.

And I want to press ahead a little bit with the old rules if I may, because I feel they haven't been getting as much of a run for their money as they might have done. Now what I mean by speaking up a bit for the old rules is that it seems to me there were virtues in relation to political practice. They may have done some mischief here and there, and insofar as they were in any way causally related—which probably shouldn't be exaggerated—to the invention of the nuclear weapon, let alone to the very clear connection between that intellectual enterprise which in a sense is given to us by the fact that it has worked, and it's puzzling to us why it should, and it's important to try to understand as well as one can why it does and doesn't.

And certainly in relation to political practice, I think an insistence on the moral virtues of honesty and insistence on the regulative role in human thinking, of the rules of logic and an insistence on trying to understand as soberly as one can why human knowing works where it does and doesn't work where it doesn't work, is obviously a precondition for actually formulating well-considered political goals, and a precondition for cementing together the very motley coalition of human interests, every single member of which has after all their own subjectivity, together to move towards those goals.

SPIVAK   I should think of that as a problem rather than a solution. It seems to me that what I was saying was not that you should consider all other subjects. I was saying that you might want to entertain the notion that you cannot consider all other subjects and that you should look at your own subjective investment in the narrative that is being produced. You see, that is something that I will continue to repeat, it is not an invitation to be benevolent towards others.

DUNN   Well, they certainly don't allow me to produce elegant solutions—I wish to God they did. I think that—you say that this modality of political—attempted political co-operation may conceal all sorts of dreadful things. My point is simply that it needn't and the question of whether it does or whether it doesn't has to be answered, as it always has had to be answered in human history, by looking and seeing whether it does or not. And I simply think that it's a false claim, a result of an overestimation of the constraining force of rhetoric. It's a false claim that the project of attempting rationally to understand human societies commits people to any form of practical political co-operation in any determinate form of oppression. I see no such link. There may be contingent links in relation to particular people—the world's a confusing place and people are often in fact involved in complicity in things, which if you pointed out to them clearly that they were, they would be pretty appalled by. But it doesn't seem to me that there's any connection at all between the project of trying to understand clearly and being committed to the doing of bad things. I simply reject the existence of any such link—as a link of necessity. These are all contingent matters and we must just look at them and make what sense we can.

SPIVAK   Yes. I'm not suggesting some kind of reflection theory, isomorphic relationship between the project of rationalism and untold crimes committed all over the world, no. I'm suggesting that you extend your idea of looking and seeing to the rationalist project as you produce it, not as others might suffer from it. I will continue to say it is an invitation for the investigating subject to see that the projects are produced within a much larger textuality.

We don't think of it as necessary, but we say that there is something like a relationship, very heterogenous, different in different fields, but one must look and see constantly, and the rationalist project should not be free of that glance.

DUNN   But of course it shouldn't be. It least of all projects should ever have suggested that it should be free. I mean, the idea of self-understanding is one of the principal human goods, as conceived within the rationalist project. So, insofar as the rationalist project as concretely, historically, been associated with and in practice produced by and indeed formed by complicity in the doing of bad things, it has betrayed itself.

SPIVAK   But the idea has failed because it has not acknowledged that self-understanding is impossible. That has been the trouble.

DUNN   Supposing we acknowledge that self-understanding is impossible. What should we do politically on the basis of that insight?

SPIVAK   Precisely what I have been suggesting. I think first of all that the Western theoretical establishment should take a moratorium on producing a global solution. It seems to me that we have been talking about—and this is why the critique of Western metaphysics is so important, as a critique of Western metaphysics in the post-structuralists. I think in the language of commercials, one would say: Try it, you might like it. Try to behave as if you are part of the margin, try to unlearn your privilege. This, I think, would be a lesson that one could draw, in a very crude way, from the post-structuralist enterprise.

DUNN   It sounds spiritually very edifying, but I'm not clear from anything you've said that it's going to be cognitively particularly helpful. And I simply don't think it is true actually that the Western intellectual establishment, whatever it is, is so full of global solutions at the moment. It seems to me to be running for cover as hard as it can go.

HAWTHORN   But Ron, you have a solution which is not exactly global but is fairly large in scale. As you listen to this conversation, what implications do you think it has for what we talked about a little earlier?

ARONSON   I think that there are probably very few non party-related Marxists today, let's say in GB and the US, who would, as you say, privilege the working class the way you were talking a few minutes ago. Rather, we've seen what, since the latter part of the 19th century—the development of imperialism, even before that forms of enslavement, various forms of racism, colonialism, imperialism, the explosions of the 20th century, the rise of the women's movement, the assault on racism— we see in other words in what is increasingly a world-wide system various layers of oppression, very different ones, various forms of struggle which people have been wrestling to grasp the intelligibility of, and which it seems to me one can begin to chart an overall intelligibility of. It seems to me it's not a matter of throwing up one's hand and saying all of these are localised and different, but rather there is still a worldwide order which has generated these various phenomena in different sectors.

Now it seems to me if we look on this history and go back far enough and come into the present, if the nuclear clock does not run to midnight, if that does not happen, rather than a negative outlook, rather than a despairing vision of our prospects, we might be able to have a much more positive one. Because we see these struggles continue to be generated, going back at least to Spartacus, and that people continue to struggle and will continue to struggle for dignity, for a decent life, for power, for freedom, for democracy, for their own integrity. And I can't see a stopping point to those struggles until they're won.

HAWTHORN   In a way he's turning the argument of the deconstructionists back on itself. He's saying that there is indeed a grand récit to be told, a story to be recounted, a cumulative story, a story which gives one a stronger and stronger sense of these movements emerging and from time to time coming to power, and even if they fail in the power they acquire, nevertheless leaving a lesson behind them.

SPIVAK   To an extent I think the post-structuralist project would look at history not as a series of brute facts but as narratives generated in one way or another. Derrida has a statement where he says that deconstruction is the deconstitution of the founding concepts of the Western historical narrative. And a small point—which can very easily be misunderstood—that in Ron's narrative, the history of resistance begins with Spartacus.

ARONSON   I said "at least."

SPIVAK   OK, the apology made, but nonetheless, there it is. There is something that we would think about there.

The point is not to recover a lost consciousness, but to see, to quote Macherey, the itinerary of the silencing. You see, that's what one looks at. So from that point of view, our view of history is a very different view. It is also cumulative, but it's a view where we see the way in which narratives compete with each other, which one rises, which one falls, who is silent, and the itinerary of the silencing rather than the retrieval. And we can also see that we ourselves are bound to narrate, which is why I quoted Lyotard's narrative in *La Condition Post Moderne*, so that one shouldn't think that we are somehow outside waging war.

ARONSON   If we were doing that kind of narrative in the US, and we were to ask the question, Who built the railroads?—in a classroom for example—one of the first answers students might give would be: the Rockefellers, or the Harrimans, and then with a bit of prodding someone might say, well, the Irish or the Chinese. And one would go through that process of starting out with the established vision, the dominant vision of how history was produced, to a vision of history being produced rather differently.

But at the end of that discussion, people might walk away saying: Now I understand who really built the railroads. It seems to me that conclusion is not a conclusion that your approach would allow.

SPIVAK   Because they didn't really build the railroads, either. The Rockefellers built it too, you see, so that to an extent what one—

ARONSON   But are you willing to then analyse the building of the railroads in terms of the various forces of capital and labour and technology, and say: We can finally decide to the best of our knowledge, reasonably objectively, that the building of the railroads took place in the following ways, and lay out various relationships between the various forces and come up with an objective interpretation.

SPIVAK   This is the only narrative we can construct, is what we can say. That is what in fact allows us to understand that we are working within limits instead of saying it's an objective analysis.

ARONSON   But are you willing to say this is the fullest possible, the most adequate, narrative? You see, I'm pushing you on the question of objectivity.

SPIVAK   At the moment?

ARONSON   Of course. I would agree with that.

SPIVAK   You know the question that Mary O'Brien asks, as you are being a critic by day and a fisherman by night, I forget quite what the day/night breakdown there is, who's minding the babies. So you see, to an extent there's always that further question, event those—so that one doesn't know, one shouldn't want to close off discussion, one should be able to say: Look, I'm putting my interests scrupulously on the table, this is what we can do at the moment, but there you are. There's no debate there, is there?

DUNN   Well one certainly shouldn't try to close off discussion. That's a very good rationalist enlightenment principle. But I think probably we are still in some fairly strong disagreement about one matter which anyway concerns us as educators if not necessarily from other points of view, which is that you say the great texts of the past are texts which speak to us because of what they shy away from or leave out. And I think from my point of view, my belief is still that the great texts of the past should speak to us because of the passages of cognitive mastery which they contain. That the heritage of the accumulated, intellectual, rationally reconsidered heritage of the history of the human race is all we have with which to think about where we find ourselves.

But the idea of deciding to stop using that, or becoming paralysed in our attempts to use it, because it's a hard business getting anywhere if you use it as vigorously as you can dare—the idea that one should accept that persuasion, because one may well be wrong, is not actually politically at all a benign persuasion. We may be wrong about very many matters. Actually, if you look at us soberly and historically and cumulatively, we must be wrong. Humans always get things wrong. But the idea that we shouldn't try to draw as systematically as we can on human thinking in its most systematic elements because that may have got, and must have got in fact, and certainly did get, tangled up with the history of human oppression—that is *not* actually an educationally benign persuasion. About that I think we really do genuinely at last disagree.

SPIVAK   I hope so. I would say that as a teacher, it seems to me that even as we work with—we all teach within certain kinds of institutions that have a certain sort of contract, so here when I say let us not close off discussion, I'm not forgetting that earlier I had said certain regimes of truth will not allow people to enter, or we can't even hear them. So I'm now speaking as your colleague.

It seems to me that in that kind of a situation the fact that the best tools that we seem to have are those tools of rational thinking, does not stop us from saying that they might be symptomatic rather than, as I said earlier, the union ticket to truth. I think there is no harm in that, especially since in these kinds of academic institutions, as I also said earlier, what is being produced—perhaps we might think they are just benign, and they're just disinterested knowledge—but what is being produced is cultural explanations that silence others.

And in terms of that mutism, for example, I have said in another context about feminism that perhaps rather than asking the question What is woman? because that—or What am I?—which would be simply reiterating the question of what is man—since all we have, as you said, is this historical account, perhaps the proper question of someone who has not been allowed to be the subject of history is to say: What is man that he was obliged to produce such a text of history? So to an extent, I suppose I agree, that is all we have.

DUNN   Well, that's quite a question, isn't it?

SPIVAK   To an extent all I'm suggesting is that one turn back on history as a production of various kinds of narratives, and that one then not offer the idea that there will be an objective analysis which will then be an end of narrativisation, because one is also caught within narrating oneself.

DUNN   But even modern philosophers of natural science don't think there's going to be an objective analysis which will be the end of narration. Nobody really thinks that any longer. And what I think we do still disagree about is—you say that any human cognitive project will terminate in a cultural explanation which silences others, and my view is that that is only true insofar as any particular human cognitive project ends up in an invalid set of conclusions.

SPIVAK   I wasn't speaking of any human cognitive project. Once again, I was very careful in establishing the fact that we are talking within certain kinds of institutional constraints. We have been trained to teach at certain kinds of institutions, that is where we teach. I even allowed myself the pleasure of saying that I was speaking as your colleague. Within that particular frame, it seems to me, out of the theoretical production, in the First World comes the cultural explanations that I'm speaking of. So once again it's not a generalised statement—although I did say that the pleasure in cognition—and there Lyotard goes back to Kant— and so does Foucault—the pleasure in cognitive victories, if understood as symptomatic, can be enabling rather than disabling. And if it is disabling, it is not a disablement that one should shy away from.

HAWTHORN   One shouldn't close off discussion, certainly, but we do live and work within an institutional context, including the context of the programme, and I'm afraid that this particular discussion must stop. But at least I hope that it's been an enabling one.

Thank you all very much.

3

Strategy, Identity, Writing

This is an edited transcript of a three-hour interview conducted in Canberra, Australia, on August 17, 1986. The participants were John Hutnyk, Scott Mc-Quire, Nikos Papastergiadis, and Gayatri Spivak. First published in Melbourne Journal of Politics, Vol. 18, 1986/87.

MJP   Let us begin by looking, in a way, to the end of the interview. What could be said about the power relations in this event?

GCS   You want me to comment on this interview? Now, in this room? Well, in a situation like this one, the hegemony is rather clearly articulated. There is one person who is supposed to have some answers, and others who ask questions, and given that questioning and answering is placed in an orthodox way, the one who answers has the power. On the other hand, since this will get transcribed and published, and given over to people, that easy articulation of the hegemonic situation is no longer operative, because the person who gets judged is the person who answers the questions, so that there is a certain kind of nervousness on the part of the person answering. This is not the situation when you're actually writing or teaching. So, paradoxically, I would say that I find my power very much less in an interview situation, than in the classroom or when I'm writing.

MJP   Can you focus more specifically on the distinction between the written and the spoken?

GCS   This distinction is an interested distinction, isn't it? As we know from Derrida, speech is structured according to those structures in writing that are generally denigrated as non-spontaneous, dead. Speech cannot, indeed, be understood if there isn't a pre-existing code which is institutional, and to conceive of the living present, the subject has to understand her own death. Any articulation of the living present in the stream of speech makes you understand that there was a 'present' before you and there will be a 'present' after you. In order to conceive of the continuity and spontaneity of the interview as speech, the speaker must irreducibly, structurally assume her absence before and after. Our access to spontaneity in speech is actually governed by those structures which one associates with writing. This is a position that Derrida has drawn

35

attention to. Speech operates by way of a code that would work in the speaker's absence.

But even within that theoretical position, I think one must in the narrow sense distinguish between speech and writing, because politically speech and writing are distinguished. And this is the difference, much more crude, much less philosophical, that I was making between speaking to you in this room, where I have a certain authority, and then the launching of the interview within the institutional context where your journal will circulate, so that the situation becomes more complicated.

People often forget that published texts are transactional. But the distinction between the written and the spoken is one of degree rather than kind. Even speaking 'off the cuff' is conditioned by a whole variety of psycho-social, ethno-economic, historical and ideological strands—all those modes of differentiation which are more or less violent in their necessary constitutive exclusions. There is a complicity between violence and discourse. Derrida at a certain point—again this is not in writing— was questioned about the relationship between epistemological phenomena and other structures of violence. On the one hand, writing does entail a certain generalised system of violence. On the other hand, there exist structures of violence in the world which cannot be reduced to just the violence of writing. He said something that stuck in my mind, that there is a constant negotiation between these two structures of violence, and whatever you call theoretical, you have to be aware that you're negotiating in one way or another.

MJP   This negotiation often spills out in our unconscious slips. . . .

GCS   Yes, what I like about interviews is that they teach me things, not only about myself, but about things I've thought, which doesn't quite happen if I take good stock of what I'm going to say. It's always interesting to see one's own slips, or, where one falls back. These are things that you don't really get in other situations.

It's a wonderful way of 'othering' oneself. I like to surrender myself to the interviews, is what I'm saying!

MJP   During the discussion of your recent paper in Melbourne you make a remark which raises interesting questions about participation in the production of knowledge. You said: 'If you find a flaw in my argument, if you find a certain problem, please use it, please lever yourself from it . . . but don't just think you can diagnose me'.

GCS   Well, this is one of the pleasures of coming to such gatherings as that in Melbourne. When someone stands up in the audience and presents some problem with what I have said, then great. I will learn, too, in that situation. At the same time, if someone says that they read in an interview I gave in 1986, something that was different to what I said in, say, 1976, I would simply say 'Too bad!'—and that is that! (Laughter.)

Don't try and bind me. Don't bind anyone. You oblige me to become aggressive, is something I would say. I am not interested in people who want only to point out faults.

MJP   In someone like Foucault, you always get this idea that knowledge is going to be a competition. Whereby you go into the market place and tell lies to each other, and there is never any kind of communication, or any attempt to look for a kind of communal or co-operative production of knowledge—which, for you, would signal very much more.

GCS   My work concerning the critique of the subject, of which I'm glad you noticed an example in that particular arena, makes it most interesting when someone points out something wrong. This is something which I obviously cannot do. Something from my text, which is beyond my control, has been given to me, by someone else. I do want to say that genuine criticisms are in fact a gift, and such offerings can change our attitude towards consolidating our own position within the academy.

MJP   You spend much of your time moving among the various academic institutions. What effect do you think travel has on your work?

GCS   Well, you know, I think for a time I will stop travelling. I became caught up in this travelling circus, and I think I've kept doing it for so long because it undermined some of the seriousness with which I was beginning to take myself. If one travels, one notices how seriously each institution takes itself! If you are travelling on all of these continents, moving from university to university, the one thing that strikes you is that each place takes itself to be the centre of the intellectual universe! (Laughter.) Even when it is defining itself in terms of other greater places, in that act of self-definition, it is its own importance that is emphasised. And that was a wonderful antidote for me. It was impossible for me to take myself seriously anymore in that sense of 'I will save the world', which begins to infect middle-aging academics when other people want to listen to them. But I think I'll stop travelling.

MJP   Has living, and writing, 'on the run' given you a further perspective on identity?

GCS   As far as I can tell, one is always on the run, and it seems I haven't really had a home base—and this may have been good for me. I think it's important for people not to feel rooted in one place. So, wherever I am, I feel I'm on the run in some way. But with this is combined the fact that I write with great difficulty in both English and Bengali. This relationship between languages compels me to recognize that neither is a natural or an artificial language. I'm devoted to my native language, but I cannot think it as natural, because, to an extent, one is never natural . . . one is never at home.

One needs to be vigilant against simple notions of identity which overlap neatly with language or location. I'm deeply suspicious of any determinist or positivist definition of identity, and this is echoed in my attitude to writing styles. I don't think one can pretend to imitate adequately that to which one is bound. So, our problem, and our solution, is that we do pretend this imitation when we write, but then must do something about the fact that one knows this imitation is not OK anymore.

MJP You often quote yourself in your writing. What is the status of this strategy?

GCS Sometimes because I think, 'Well, I said it better in that other article', and so I pull it forward. But it is more than that. There's lots of cross-hatchings and interruptions. If one looks at what one has done, from the distance, then it seems to me that like everyone else I am absolutely plural.

That is in a general sense. At the same time I have inherited a certain history—born in metropolitan Bengal, having a post-colonial education, gaining expertise in European matters, and also, being and becoming a Marxist. There is this development; becoming more European in European matters than Europeans, because of survival necessity mixed with certain kinds of post-colonial pride, first generation of young intellectuals after independence, all of that Marxist training which is slowly transforming from the first internationalist waves, having left and then lived through the American sixties, first as a student, then as a teacher, and so on. I find that I'm still learning and unlearning so much that the earlier things that I've written become interpretable to me in new ways. Perhaps this happens to everyone, but I don't see marks of this in other people's writing so much. And I think repeating myself in that way keeps me aware that one is always on the move, always citational in one way or another. If you like, in the narrow sense, it is to mark the place of one's own citationality.

MJP So quoting yourself is both a mark of passage and a reference to a particular representative space?

GCS I mean, this entire movement, the itinerary of this learning and unlearning process, has me as a vehicle citing an earlier history. And I emphasise different aspects according to the political context. With the Hindu Brahmin birth and independence, and all of that . . . I mean, it is with such big and visible card-carrying moments in history that one learns to recognise, with fascination, that little sense of a self that has shown up in one's own intellectual and political production.

MJP   Can you explain this by saying how important 'India' is for you? Can you expand upon the differentiation within your 'Indian' background?

GCS   I don't write a great deal about 'India', but I am very happy that it's placed within quotation marks here. 'India', for people like me, is not really a place with which they can form a national identity because it has always been an artificial construct. 'India' is a bit like saying 'Europe'. When one is talking about a European identity, for example, one is obviously reacting against the United States.

MJP   Or when one says 'the Third World' or 'Asia'.

GCS   Yes. And 'Indian-ness' is not a thing that exists. Reading Sanskrit scriptures, for example—I can't call that Indian, because after all, India is not just Hindu. That 'Indic' stuff is not India. The name India was given by Alexander the Great by mistake. The name Hindustan was given by the Islamic conquerors. The name Bharat, which is on the passport, is in fact a name that hardly anyone uses, which commemorates a mythic king. So it isn't a place that we Indians can think of as anything, unless we are trying to present a reactive front, against another kind of argument. And this has its own contradictions.

For example, when I'm constructing myself as an Indian in reaction to racism, I am very strongly taking a distance from myself. If an Indian asks me what I am, I'm a Bengali, which is very different.

MJP   It seems India is often positioned as the 'other' of the West.

GCS   Yes, but I am not happy with this. Part of my work is to notice what kinds of distinctions were made among the so-called others of the West. I have used the example of the codification of law. In this situation the Islamic code was taken as a real code, since it was a monotheistic code, but it was seen as incorrect. The Hindu code was taken as a real code, since it was within the Indo-European code, but become monstrous, because it was polytheistic—it had to be restored through various European codes and the British Commonwealth. And anything that was not either Hindu or Muslim—tribals and so on, and in a wider context, non-Islamic Africa and the Aboriginals of Australia—did not have a code, and was made the place of magic and fetishism. It is in this kind of context that one has to see the othering of the other of the West, in actual imperial practice. The other of the West, in this hegemonic practice, was not subjected to simple racism, it was also divided in various kinds of ways.

I think we should also look at the West as differentiated. I'm really not that moved by arguments for homogenisation on both sides.

MJP   According to Ashis Nandy, one of the features of the Hindu mentality is its ability to incorporate difference, without implying assimilation. This is not homogenisation, but an implication that cultures can co-exist beside each other and also interact without displacing their fundamental dynamics.

GCS   Ashis and I are both pretty much products of the nineteenth century version of Hinduism, which developed in certain ways alongside cultural imperialism. I find it difficult to talk about the Hindu mentality, and things like that, but there is no doubt there are ways in which I'm constituted as someone who was born a Hindu which are beyond my grasp. If there is such a thing in Hinduism which assimilates in this way, perhaps it's because it was originally without a centralised focus, and so survived through dispersion. This multi-levelled aspect of Hinduism I find quite interesting.

But then, I also find myself shrinking back from those definitions of the Hindu mentality which can lead to a nineteenth century vision of nationalism. Any kind of apologetics for Hinduism coming today from Indians like myself has to take note that one of the most politically pernicious phenomena in India, and also in the United States, is Hindu fundamentalism. So, from this particular perspective, it is strategically less good to produce ways in which Hinduism had it better than so-called 'post-Enlightenment Christian humanism'.

On the other hand, I was brought up in the Kali worshipping sect whose central figure is a woman. Although I'm not in favour of those French feminist psycho-analytic suggestions that if only one could bring Kali into Lacan—since Kali is a hegemonic female—one could have a feminist psychoanalysis. I find that really rather boring. Nonetheless, helped by other people who have actually made this analysis, I have found myself quite deeply involved with pictures of female violence which the Kali sect found normal. I must say I'm not particularly pleased at having been told that that's where this positive female image comes from. But I think this has stuck, so that I can define myself as an 'ideologically interpolated' shakto—a shakto being a person from the Kali worshipping sect, shakti being the noun—if I have to define myself in any way.

MJP   A word that has often been associated with you and that you have had to react against is marginal. Could you elaborate your position on marginality?

GCS   I find the demand on me to be marginal always amusing. And as I have said, I'm tired of dining out on being an exile because that has a long tradition and it is not one I want to identify myself with. But the question is a more complex one. In a certain sense, I think there is nothing that is central. The centre is always constituted in terms of its own marginality. However, having said that, in terms of the hegemonic historical narrative, certain peoples have always been asked to cathect the margins so others can be defined as central. Negotiating between these two structures, sometimes I have to see myself as the marginal in the eyes of others.

In that kind of situation the only strategic thing to do is to absolutely present oneself at the centre. And this is theoretically incorrect. But one of the things I've said about deconstruction is that none of its examples can match its discourse. If I can't keep my hands theoretically clean anyway, why not take the centre when I'm being asked to be marginal? I'm never defined as a marginal in India, I can assure you.

MJP   In your work you have challenged the phallic metaphors through which gender roles are constructed and questioned the stereo-typical positions which are often considered binding.

GCS   Well, I don't know. I think the extent of this embrace can often be overstated. To say, for example, that we are in a cleft stick, now that's not very phallic in itself. I seems to me—you said your questions were all entangled in each other, my answers are too—that since one is obliged to produce knowledge, one should perhaps clean up the metaphorical situation moment by moment, that is to say, in a certain persistent way. There's a lot of stuff about gripping and grasping in description of appropriation through knowledge. In fact, if people would simply think upon it, it is a feminine metaphor. In the missionary position, she gets a grip upon his thighs. I'm quoting from a play of Yeats', where the mad woman sings a song about her inability to grasp the human reality of political martyrs as not being able to 'get a grip upon his thighs'. What about just simply looking at the ways in which—in my case from a dominantly heterosexist, feminine point of view—one could re-inscribe these very same metaphors . . . infiltrate them?

MJP   Can we clean up metaphor?

GCS   No. It's like cleaning teeth. You know, you will never be able to clean your teeth once and for all. But cleaning one's teeth, keeping oneself in order, etc.—it's not like writing books. You don't do these things once and for all. That's why it should be persistent.

MJP   So political practice is like housework?

GCS   And who doesn't know this? Except political theorists who are opining from the academy with theological solutions once and for all. I mean, political practice is more complex than housework, but, to take the example of the metaphorical arena, it involves the same persistent effort. Because you are inserted in an inherited vocabulary, putting in heterosexist, feminist metaphors is important, but not enough. We must be conscious of this whilst we are engaged in other things; it can't become our central goal just to keep watching our language.

MJP   You have spoken of the importance of restoring woman to the position of the questioning subject and suggest replacing the old problem 'What is woman?' with the question 'What is man that the itinerary of his desire creates such a text?'

GCS   Now, immediately the initial question about the interview situation takes on another answer. It's the questioning subject that one wants to be! (Laughter.) You are the questioning subject here, so there goes our first description of the power situation.

MJP   So the challenge is not just to reverse the content and order of categories, but rather to question the formation of structures.

GCS   In a certain way, yes! When I was talking about putting woman in the position of the questioning subject, I was really thinking more about the context of phallocentrism. It was a critique of the discourse of woman as produced, as defined by men. I hoped that it would be more interesting if we could take for ourselves the position of the questioning subject, not just 'Who am I as a woman?' but that question about man in terms of the text produced. But since then, I've moved on a little, since I now think about the arena of practice in a somewhat broader way. It also seems to me, now, that the women who can in fact begin to engage in this particular 'winning back' of the position of the questioning subject, are in very privileged positions in the geopolis today. So, from that point of view, I would not say that as a woman that my particular enemy is the male establishment of the most privileged Western tradition. They are my enemy in the house where I give interviews, where I teach, and so on, but the house of the world is much bigger than that little house. I have gained an entry there, and there I have to talk about winning the position.

But, I can also take myself more seriously as a woman, now, since I have graduated out of just that perception of the fight, where I was clearly one who was not winning. One must be conscious of the struggle to win back the position of the questioning subject in specific context. But if I think in terms of the much larger female constituency in the world for whom I am an infinitely privileged person, in this broader context, what I really want to learn about is what I have called the unlearning of one's privilege. So that, not only does one become able to listen to that other constituency, but one learns to speak in such a way that one will be taken seriously by that other constituency. And furthermore, to recognize that the position of the speaking subject within theory can be an historically powerful position when it wants the other actually to be able to answer back. As a feminist concerned about women, that's the position that interests me more.

MJP   This is where you say, in the preface to Mahasweta Devi's stories, 'We'll not be able to speak to women out there if we depend

completely on conferences and anthologies by Western-trained informants'. What are you trying to set up? A new speaking place?

GCS I have no idea what I'm trying to say about this particular problem. I don't have a very specific answer yet. I don't see my way clear,
because I don't think one can deny history quite so easily. This is a very
difficult undertaking, and it also seems to me that I'll probably not
succeed in it. On the other hand, I compare myself here sometimes to
my white male students, who complain that they can no longer speak.
I say to them that they should develop a degree of rage against a history
that has allowed that, that has taken away from them the possibility of
speaking. To an extent, in the context of women at large, that's the kind
of bind that one's in. I have no theoretical models for what one should
develop, because this is my problem—I'm speaking of myself as a representative of a certain kind of feminist—and my problem is not the important problem here. So if I were to try to produce a new speech, etc., I
would still really not be of any interest to the kind of people I'm thinking
about. To an extent, the solution of this one is going to come from
elsewhere. I'm not trying to pre-empt that because I could appropriate
it only too easily.

MJP How, then, can one problematise the authority and the role of
the investigating subject?

GCS It seems to me that this problem is different in different situations. The institutionalisation of the investigating subject is not generally
the same in every way, and in fact, quite often, new positions are secured
for the previously marginal, so that I don't think I could give you an
overall answer as to *how* one problematises. The one way—now that I've
said I can't answer it generally—it seems to me, is by researching the
historical institutionalization of specific subject positions. The ways in
which history has been narrativised always secures a certain kind of
subject position which is predicted on marginalising certain areas. The
importance of deconstruction is its interest in such strategic exclusions.
In a certain species of deconstructive 'criticism', for example, what is
being excluded is what used to be called, in the old days, the content. If
one were to look at this deconstructively, one would perhaps see why
Derrida suggests that deconstruction in the long run will encounter the
same problems as empiricism, distinguished only by that one trick which
is a certain version of 'awareness'. You know that you can't just keep
with one side of a binary opposition, you can't form constantly regressive
positions here in terms of the subject position, because then what you're
ignoring is the other side. You're excluding, in fact, the content-oriented
problems because they're not philosophical enough. And that's where
the historical research into the narrativisation and institutionalisation of
the subject position becomes very important.

Because it is a way of continuing to investigate substantive problems whilst trying to think through the problem of infinite regression, of never being able to finally ground a theoretical form. This recognizes what I now call interruptions—all of a sudden becoming aware that, in fact, there is an infinite regress on the margins of your substantive work. It's a genuine interruption in that it is discontinuous with the substantive concerns, but it is itself interrupted by bringing oneself back to the substantive investigation. All this might be another way of saying: 'You must begin where you are'.

MJP   How can you relate this theory of interruption to everyday practice?

GCS   As we talk about the practicing subject in this way, it sounds very abstract, but if you start doing things in this way, you see it keeps the whole thing moving in a much more inclusive way. The old style relied, on the one hand, on always chopping off that part of the substance regarded as not relevant, or, on the other hand, ignoring the substance and concentrating only on the structure of our practice, and the impossibility of ever watching this structure to its end. We are trying to get around that kind of binary opposition between form and content in proposing this interruption structure.

Theory always norms practice. When you practice, as it were, you construct a theory and irreducibly the practice will norm the theory, rather than be an example of indirect theoretical application. What I'm more interested in now is the radical interruption of practice by theory, and of theory by practice, and to an extent my inability to produce a quick answer is because it's a genuine interruption. If what I'm thinking about, in terms of the different feminist practice, were not a real interruption, then I would be able to accommodate it, consolidate it, appropriate it, define it, produce models of newspeak and so on, and be home free. But the nature of an interruption is that it really does put a monkey wrench in the whole thing. It is a genuine discontinuity.

MJP   How would this relate to a political semiotic program and what you call disruption of the sign system?

GCS   What we are doing is examining the production of sign systems and what I find interesting is what Derrida said in the early days, that we cannot get away from the structure of the sign. That's why we have to look at the ways in which we are bound in it. This is the real problem.

MJP   In your article in Subaltern Studies, volume four, you quote Derrida: 'The enterprise of deconstruction always in a certain way falls prey to its own work'. You add: 'This is the greatest gift of deconstruction'. Would you expand on the two judgments, and the apparent paradox.

GCS   The reason why I say it is the greatest gift is that, although I make a specific use of deconstruction, I'm not a deconstructivist. Once you are aware that the only way in which you can deconstruct is by making the structure of that which you critique the structure of your own criticism, then you become conscious of the limitations of total escape. The kind of use I make of deconstruction is this resolute stand against the vanguardism of theory. If you escape in the end, you lose. I think that the greatest problem with theoretical production has been its sense of being right.

MJP   Is this dilemma basic to the ambivalence of whether Derrida is engaged in a positive or negative science?

GCS   Yes, and it seems to me also that the mature Derrida talks about being willy-nilly engaged in a positive science, and since deconstruction cannot be a positive science, what it produces is a kind of critical ballast to that which the philosopher, or the critic, or the political person, or the theorist, must engage in. Deconstruction says to us over and over again that it is not possible to have positive sciences—on the other hand, it is always abundantly possible! Since one cannot not be an essentialist, why not look at the ways in which one is essentialist, carve out a representative essentialist position, and then do politics according to the old rules whilst remembering the dangers in this? That's the thing that deconstruction gives us; an awareness that what we are obliged to do, and must do scrupulously, in the long run is not OK. But this is not, and could not be, a political theory. So I don't see this as a dilemma. Or, if it is a dilemma, it's the dilemma that also gives you a solution.

MJP   Is this actually just saying that deconstruction is aware that it can never pretend to present a final and total position? If so, why should we apologise for this?

GCS   Well, I am not apologising. But, on the other hand, it's also the kind of thinking which puts being aware into question. That is to say, being aware is produced as a kind of symptom, in defence against all kinds of other things. So the fact that as a person influenced by deconstruction I'm aware of this, is certainly not particularly a great assurance. In any case, deconstruction does present final and total positions, because it is not possible to avoid presenting final and total positions. Even if you just want to make your arguments stick for the next half an hour, the positions that you presuppose will be final and total positions. But there is a kind of safety valve which says, 'Do not make them universal'.

MJP   It is a question of what sort of finality you impose on your own perspective.

GCS   Well, the question that really comes to my mind is What is perspective? There are all these 'eye' metaphors! A perspective is a glass, right? It's like a spectacle through which you see everything. Now we also talk about the position that one is in. Perspective is something that you have to articulate—I mean, in terms of my political position, for example, I would say that you have to clear a representative space for yourself, because there is no way that you can, in fact, not speak from a place. And you can't just dismiss it by saying, 'This was only perspectival', because you must think of that perspective as, in fact, finally viable, otherwise it's being naive. You cannot freely play. This is one of the things that deconstruction also teaches us. If one does start, self-consciously, to engage in free play, once again one makes a very deterministic mistake, thinking that the narrating can adequately represent the philosophy. Thinking that we can exactly imitate the notions of deconstruction by engaging in a little bit of free play. For even as we are supposed to be 'freely playing', we are finalising the situation out of which we are speaking. Derrida said, at a certain point—I don't think this is in print—'Deconstruction is not exposure of error, it is a vigilance about the fact that we are always obliged to produce truth'. You know, this is the thing that is striking about it. It's not some kind of a negative metaphysical caper because there's nothing positive in the world; it's an examination, over and over again, of the fact that we are obliged to produce truths, positive things, we are obliged to finalize, perspectives must be generalised, and so on. . . .

MJP You have written that deconstruction cannot provide the basis for a political program. Yet in various notes throughout your work you qualify for this. For example: 'I believe it is possible to read in this obscure text [Derrida's "On an Apocalyptic Tone Recently Adopted in Philosophy"] a practical politics of the open end.' What did you mean?

GCS Well, that last statement, to an extent doesn't go with what I have said elsewhere about affirmative deconstruction, but I'll explain. In 1980, at a conference on Derrida's work, there was a very moving—since Derrida isn't dead, it's not possible to say eulogy, but, it was a thing like that—there was a wonderful account, in Derrida's presence, of his own work, in very reverent terms. And then Derrida stood up after the talk, and he said well, thank you, and so on, and, on the other hand, there is a difference between what I'm up to now, and what you have so carefully described. He said that the first wave of my work, I was interested in 'garder la question', in keeping the question alive. Whenever something happens, don't forget that it can be questioned. But what I'm doing now is an 'appel à tout-autre', it's the call to the wholly other, which is different from keeping the question alive. And my own feeling has been that it was when he became interested in questions of sexual difference, around 1974, that this change came about. In an essay on *La carte postale*, which came out in *Diacritics*, I did talk about how the figure of the woman works in Derrida. Now, when he went into affirmative deconstruction, I think what he began to realise is not that you have to say no to whatever positive stuff you're doing, that is to say 'keeping the question alive'. But that deconstruction obliges you to say yes to everything. You have to say yes to that which interrupts your project. And in terms of that, you can't have a political program which doesn't say no to something. So, a political program cannot base itself upon affirmative deconstruction, because then it will very quickly come to resemble pluralism, and I think pluralism, as a political program, has already shown its dark side, especially in the United States. I think that that's what happens if affirmative deconstruction is made into a political program. On the other hand, when you are within the political program, choosing from among the yeses the possibility of saying yes to something which interrupts you does bring an end to the vanguardism of theory. That is what I meant by that footnote. It's a responsibility to the trace of the other in the self. But then you haven't based yourself on affirmative deconstruction. Politics is assymetrical, it is provisional, you have broken the theory, and that's the burden you carry when you become political.

There's a little footnote in *La double séance* talking about literature where Derrida says: 'But of course there is no way one can distinguish between literature and something else because that part of your opposition is not viable'. On the other hand, he says that *that* way of 'being deconstructive' would neutralise all kinds of oppositions. Therefore, what one has to look at is how historically some things have been *called* literature, and others have not been. And then, in fact, you're not being deconstructive, you are being asymmetrical, you have broken the program. A program of deconstruction can't be followed. It stays there as a marker of the limit to the power of knowledge. It is not itself a counter-program for the production of knowledge.

MJP   Well, how do you react to Greg Ulmer's book *Applied Grammatology* and that whole challenge to established forms of pedagogy and discipleship?

GCS   I think the book is interesting. But there are problems with undermining discipleship via grammatology. For a start there's the immense problem of already having the negative metaphysics on the ground and deconstruction feeding into it. Because these kind of things, when they are chained in this way, when their disruptive power is domesticated, become incorporated into what is already there. Just as in the hands of Michael Ryan and Terry Eagleton, it begins to resemble ideology critique, or in the hands of the free-playing enthusiasts, begins to resemble negative metaphysics, I must, with respect, say that the pedagogic program that Ulmer was laying out resembles nothing so much as a sort of 1960s boys-and-girls-playing-together participatory etiquette. That sort of game playing really cannot operate except in very privileged circumstances. And that's the sort of thing that I'm most afraid of, because, as I was saying, learning from the other side, where real reactionaries hang out, there are obvious ways in which it can just be dismissed as yet another attitude. Whether or not a deconstructive morphology can be used in a pedagogical situation depends very much upon your constituency and discerning how the power lines, the ethnoclass divisions of the student population are breaking in that institutional space.

MJP   So what you're really criticizing is canonizing it without regard to specific context?

GCS   Yes, and especially when it starts resembling progressive teaching, because it doesn't undermine discipleship. As I said two years ago in Melbourne, the discourses against watershed intellectuals, in fact, have been taken up as discourse given by watershed intellectuals. Cutting around discipleship is not so easy. We begin to get disciples of nondiscipleship.

MJP   What are you doing now?

GCS   Where am I? Well, I'm supposedly revising a manuscript called 'Master Discourse, Native Informant: Deconstruction in the Service of Reading' . . . I'm not a book writer, I'm very unhappy about the fact that I have finally had to perpetrate a book, but that's that.

MJP   Is that a deliberate strategy, though? To be an essayist rather than a book writer?

GCS   I don't know that it's a deliberate strategy, it's possible that I've made a virtue out of necessity. I'm afraid of writing books, because I've found myself changing my mind so much, I don't particularly like what I write . . . But nevertheless I think the time has come to take the plunge. And then there's a—this is even worse—there's a collection of essays coming out—my old essays, indeed—and it's got a very very grandiose title, it's called *In Other Worlds: Essays in Cultural Politics.* That's coming out. I've been working on a book on Derrida for a long, long time, and I have seven or eight chapters written of that, that I hope will be finished sooner or later. After that, you know, I don't know what I want to do, because my real project is the one I was talking about, but I don't see how that can be fitted into an academic context. I find myself moving more and more toward India, because that's the one place where . . . I work somewhat in Hong Kong, but I work more in India, because there I have a certain entry into the academy on the other side of the international division of labour, but I find it a little troubling because I am Indian; I mean, one would think that that would be a helpful thing, but I don't find it a helpful thing. I'd much rather it wasn't my so-called 'home'.

I have a project in mind which will also take a long time; which is on the constitution of diasporic Indians, because of the phenomenon of the United States Indians, which is the only colored community that came through the brain drain, now being used as alibis for affirmative action, and so on, and very different from the Afro-Carribean Indian diaspora or the Indian community in Britain. I want, obviously, to do it in terms of the kinds of theoretical interests I have. But that's a long project, too. I'm letting myself go a little right now. I've been teaching and writing for a long time. There are a few things in the offing. I have to do a forum on the new historicism in December. I have to do various kinds of things. I'll be teaching in India from January to June, I'll be reading Hegel with a group in Calcutta in July. I'll be doing a really funny thing in July also, which is talking in Cambridge, England, to teachers of English from the Commonwealth countries, by which is meant, of course, our dusky brethren, about the latest developments in First World theories. So, there are these odd things, but I don't really have a massive project that I can talk on. Let's end here. Thanks?

4

The Problem of
Cultural Self-representation

This interview between Gayatri Spivak and Walter Adamson was recorded in 1986 and was first published in Thesis Eleven, *No. 15, 1986. Questions on behalf of* Thesis Eleven *were formulated by Philipa Rothfield and Sneja Gunew, posed by Walter Adamson and edited by Philipa Rothfield.*

WA   Since you are interested in the strategy of reading rather than in recovering the writer's "original vision", why couldn't your approach be called a "reader response approach"? What are your reservations regarding reader response theories?

GS   The kind of reader response theory that is in vogue here in the United States seems to suggest that one could assume a community of readers without troubling to look at the socio-political production of these communities or questioning the notion of hegemonic communities. The question that I have to pose when people ask me to distinguish my position of "interest" from reader response is: who is the reader? My position vis-à-vis reader response is reactive: the political element comes out in the transaction between the reader and the texts. What I am most insistent upon is that the politics or the critic of the reader should be put on the table as scrupulously as possible. Textual criticism cannot just be a judgement on the basis of disinterested readings by a presumed community.

WA   It sounds to me as if your criticism of contemporary reader response theory is a criticism about its failure to live up to its own promise. Couldn't your own political reading incorporate reader response criticism as well as more traditional strategies of looking at the politics in the text?

GS   Yes. In fact in Eastern Germany there is a variety of reader response theory which is trying to take this into account. But when that phrase—"Reader Response Theory"—is invoked here in the U.S., we generally retreat from the question of interested political readings.

WA   Why don't we move to the question of whether or not there is an essentialism involved when we posit binary oppositions like book-author or individual-history.

GS   It seems to me that the first opposition, that between book and author, has been used to exculpate the author, saying that it is the book we are dealing with and not the author. Or the opposition can operate so as to prove the author's transcendence of history. That's the first opposition. The second opposition on the other hand, between individual and history, has been used either to assert the unquestioned shaping role of the individual as undivided consciousness or to separate that consciousness out as a text, where everything else becomes context. When I talk about those two oppositions and say that I am using them strategically, I do so knowing that in general these are essentialist problems that arise when these binary oppositions are used. But it is not possible, within discourse, to escape essentializing somewhere. The moment of essentialism or essentialization is irreducible. In deconstructive critical practice, you have to be aware that you are going to essentialize anyway. So then strategically you can look at essentialisms, not as descriptions of the way things are, but as something that one must adopt to produce a critique of anything. This gesture on the part of the critic relates to the two oppositions in two different ways.

When we operate with the opposition book-author, we want to avoid the kind of simple reversal whereby the critic's hands remain clean and the critic becomes diagnostic in a simple symptomatic reading. We keep ourselves within the book's field and see how far we can go when we respect that. In the second case, the individual and history, we want to see the individual consciousness as a crucial part of the effect of being a subject, which is itself a part of a much larger structure, one which is socio-political, politico-economic, psycho-sexual. Now all of these elements are discontinuous with each other so that you can't easily translate from the one to the other. But, nonetheless, all of these things are organised as narratives which reflect a sort of weave of presence and absence. As a result of this, you lose the confidence of *having* something which is *causing* something or *controlling* something. And from this point of view the question what is that whole thing, the whole network, no longer remains pertinent except in the context of the universalizing subject of knowledge.

In fact, Perry Anderson's recent critique of post-structuralism, *In the Tracks of Historical Materialism*, is a good example of this. He looks at the network of textuality as a continuous weave, himself tacitly assuming the position of that universalizing subject. He then proves that post-structuralism was an inevitable development from structuralism and that the two movements posited relationships between subject and structure, individual and history that entailed each other. We see this in the light of a graspable whole network and this as a kind of necessary trajectory. The pertinent chapter ends with the assertion that the question answers itself. That would in itself be symptomatic of the kind of danger that we are trying to avoid, the essentialist danger, where you translate all of the elements within that larger structure into a kind of continuous configuration which the knowing subject can control.

WA   The next obvious question, to allow you to say more about your own view of the critical process, is to ask you how to advance the process towards a feministly interested reading. Obviously there must be as many answers to that question as there are feminists. What's yours?

GS   I don't know what a feminist looks for. To an extent, my gesture towards the text is a very old-fashioned one. I think that the critic's first task is to attend to the text. So that I try, knowing that of course it's impossible to suspend myself, as it were. Having said this, I would add that my interests now, to an extent, are to be seen as: in what way, in what contexts, under what kinds of race and class situations, gender is used as what sort of signifier to cover over what kinds of things. It really is a discovery which arises through actually attending to texts. So I'm a little wary of trying to locate a program with which one actually confronts a text. I think the preparation of the critic takes place, to an extent, before the confrontation with the text just as much as with it.

WA   It seems that your view of the critical process, at least as you've articulated it so far, is as much an education of the critic as it is the critic's education of the reader. Do you also think that literary criticism can be a kind of, let's say, feminist literary guerrilla warfare towards the readers?

GS   I suppose it can be. But then again, would one have to assume a sort of "kneecapping" position, as if women are history transcendent? Of course there is a sort of euphoria in that. But, nonetheless, I think as a long-term proposition, it won't last in the wash. Guerrilla warfare takes place where guerrilla warfare takes place, and that's not academic literary criticism.

WA   Let me move on to your concept of the fractured semiotic field. In what sense is the world a semiotic field? And what do you mean by fracturing?

GS   I don't think that the world is a semiotic field. By semiotic field I had meant something as simple as this: that there are collections of axioms in the socius, depending on your position within the socius, and these axioms are by no means unified all over the globe. What I was suggesting was that when a writer writes, she doesn't just write in English or French, she also writes in these so-called sign systems, and it's in this sense that one can see the socius as a very heterogeneous collection of what I called, I think now somewhat wrongly, semiotic fields. With respect to the notion of fracture, what I am talking about is obviously the problem of cultural self-representation. The way in which semiotic fields are tapped for cultural self-representation, in fact, always covers over the dislocation between the kinds of axiomatics that are being used, and whatever it is in the "culture" that constitutes the hidden agenda of the suppression of ideological production. Let me say that very broadly-speaking, the fracture goes either in the direction of Utopianism, or in the direction of a golden-age complex. One sees the best example at festivals. And one of my favourite examples is how, at Fourth of July picnics, the United States, which is, after all, a micro-electronic capitalism, represents itself as engaging in independent commodity production. That's what I would call a fractured semiotic field. But if you say something is a semiotic field, you're suggesting that it is nothing but a text, nothing but language, nothing but words and meanings. I wasn't trying to reduce hard reality to nothing but signs. I was talking about the fact that, within the practice of representation, which is defined within the enclosure named the aesthetic, this is one strategy of tracking the socio-economic; by noticing in what way and through the covering over of what fractures, semiotic fields are being tapped.

WA   You say that you don't want to identify hard reality with the production of meaning within semiotic fields. What do you fear is missed in doing so?

GS   I'm very interested in a persistently critical practice and I think that, once one has unrecognized totalizing impulses, one can end up privileging one's own disciplinary practice. I'm not suggesting that there is a necessarily hard reality out there. In fact I would argue the opposite, that it is always dredged up as a slogan. But I would also not want to identify such reality with the production of signs. Something else *might* be going on. The concept of the sign itself, after all, is something which has emerged within certain kinds of disciplinary practices.

WA   It seems that the signifier "man" does more than float. It disguises itself under an unproblematic cover, the signifier "human". Can you say something about anthropomorphism and the concept of man as historically independent?

GS   When Derrida criticized Sartre's anthropomorphic re-reading of Heidegger, that critique of anthropomorphism was picked up in two ways, and over the last almost twenty years, we've seen it going in two directions within the deconstructive establishment. One has been for the critic to say, "Do not look in it for a *human* story, but rather for the text's constitution of its own textuality or narrativity." Another, which has been Derrida's track, has been to say: "Look here, it is almost as if the sign, anthropos, has no history." Perhaps that was what led him to say that one might look at the sign, woman, rather than simply say, "Get the human out of the way and look at the text's constitution of its own narrative." It was from that point onwards that he started worrying about the sign, woman.

WA   Could you comment on the relationship between ideology and literary criticism, or ideology and the social world, both as a battle for domination and in relation to critical readings by literary critics?

GS   I think there's a real problem when the critic of ideology takes a diagnostic position and forgets that she is herself caught within structural production. This obviously brings us to the ghost of Althusser, because the other side of the critic's taking a diagnostic position is a symptomatic reading. I think when Althusser speaks of ideology having no history, he was really writing as a philosopher and was suggesting that we think ideology before we can think history. I also think that Althusser was ill-served there by turning to Lacan in order to develop his notion of the primacy of interpellation and so on. In Lacan, what he found, after all, was still a discussion that was caught within the notions of the subject and the patronymic, the name of the father. If one looks at the current Derrida, who talks about the auto-position of the subject saying yes to itself before the possibility of discourse, I think one can use that as a lever to lift Althusser's text. One thinks ideology before one can think history as something out there, before one can, in in fact, conceive of the fact that history is the narrativizations of various kinds that are in a field of contention. When, within specific readings, people universalize one or another ideology, that, I think, has very little to do with what Althusser was trying to say. Althusser was using a kind of argumentative grid which was not sufficient to the power of his insight. He did keep on saying that one must continually re-think the distinctions between ideology and history, ideology and science, ideology and philosophy, and he finally came out recommending a *pratique sauvage*, a wild practice, a wild philosophy. It seems to me that we have the task of re-inscribing the Althusserian insight there, rather than throwing him away as a closet idealist.

WA   You say that we have the task of re-inscribing Althusser. Does part of that project involve determining the production of the text in the last instance, in Engels' phrase?

GS   I'm very glad you mention Engels. The problem is that determination, as a critique of causality, has been transformed into determinism as the fixing of causes disguised as the final instance. In his *Science of Logic*, Hegel was trying to speak about determination as the possibility of the inauguration of discourse, as we would say today perhaps the inauguration of philosophy. It is certainly a critique of causality that Hegel is advancing. To transform that into determinism has done a great deal of harm. The way I would read Althusser is to look at the notion of relative autonomy and see how, if one really thinks it through, it is looking at discursive practices—let's call it political, economic and ideo-logical—which cannot be translated one into the other in a continuous way. If one looks at it like that, then one can even go beyond the notion of many determinations, political, economic, ideological—you name it, Marxist, feminist, anti-imperialist—one can even take it into the notion of over determination as speaking of discontinuous determinations. We are in the process of throwing away that complex notion of relative autonomy, rather than using it practically, because we are being operated upon by a cultural politics of the transformation of a critique of causality into something that is the most iron-clad philosophy of causality. It seems to me that in Marx, the relationship between consciousness and materiality, or the final determining role of the economic, remain power-ful moments of bafflement that one can work at. But in the context of a fundamentalist notion of reading, we're in the process of misunderstand-ing that, misappropriating it by virtue of the particular fracture between determination as critique of causality and determinism as a re-inscription of causality.

WA   What I find confusing is the way you adeptly fuse what I have always regarded as two very different discourses, semiotics and Marx-ism. In the latter, of course, we're concerned with the relationship of being and consciousness, and in the former we're concerned with the relationship of language and society, and those two don't necessarily fuse very easily. You were speaking of fractured semiotic fields. Is it worthy of our interest to attempt to determine the causes of the fracturing of the semiotic field or is it enough simply to locate the manner in which the semiotic field is fractured?

GS   I'm a very eclectic person. I use what comes to hand. I'm not a fundamentalist. And I'm not an Althusserian in the strict sense. I'm more interested in opening up texts than in establishing, like some medieval scholar, the authenticity of a text. Within literary criticism, quite often an interdisciplinary practice means nothing more than neutralizing the vocabulary from another discipline and taking it to describe yet once again what happens between reader and text. Psychoanalysis certainly has suffered in this way. Similarly, quite often you'll see that value production, for example, is taken as an analogy for linguistic production. One ought to remember Marx's caution in the *Grundrisse*, that it would be a mistake to make an analogy between the production of value and the production of language. From my point of view, it would be much more interesting to see what happens as literature, the literary text, is completely inserted into the circuit of the production of commodities. That's how we get our best-seller lists, and what gets remaindered, what gets written, what the construction of readership is, and so on. It would be much more interesting from my point of view to see how, when that is happening, the literary artist begins to say over and over again that literature produces use value. There is a fractured semiosis if you like. The whole notion of the creative imagination comes in as literature gets into the circuit of commodity production in the most brutal sense. That, to me, is a more interesting way of using Marxism within literary criticism than constantly making analogies between literary production and the production of value.

WA   Of course, a major preoccupation for Marxists is the advancement of the proletariat. I would agree with you that we have to give up the concept of a unified subject, as Marx has it in the proletariat and other people have in patriarchy or whatever. How is it possible to speak coherently for and about marginalized groups once we give up this concept?

GS   When I criticized Foucault in my talk in Melbourne, I was not suggesting that Foucault himself had not brilliantly tried to represent the oppressed. What I was looking at in the late Foucault was the theorization of that project as letting the oppressed speak for himself. It seemed to me that theorizing in the late Foucault actually buys into the privileging of "concrete experience", which is something that is also used by the other side, by capitalism. There is an impulse among literary critics and other kinds of intellectuals to save the masses, speak for the masses, describe the masses. On the other hand, how about attempting to learn to speak in such a way that the masses will not regard as bullshit. When I think of the masses, I think of a woman belonging to that 84% of women's work in India, which is unorganized peasant labour. Now if I could speak in such a way that such a person would actually listen to me and not dismiss me as yet another of those many colonial missionaries, that would embody the project of unlearning about which I've spoken recently. What can the intellectual do toward the texts of the oppressed? Represent them and analyze them, disclosing one's own positionality for other communities in power. Foucault has done this. In fact, I can't think of another person, another intellectual, who had done this in our time in the Western context. What I was objecting to was that theorization of letting Pierre Riviere speak for himself, and what the theoretical articulation does for the people who are influenced by Foucault, enthusiastic academic intellectuals, who at the same time swallow Foucault's critique of the watershed intellectual and make Foucault into a watershed intellectual!

WA   Does speaking to marginalized groups and yet not "deskilling" oneself mean anything about the kinds of texts that one ought to speak about?

GS   When I sad that one shouldn't invite people to de-skill themselves, I was talking about a kind of anti-intellectualism that exists among
academics and counter-academics. One ought not to patronize the oppressed. And that's where this line leaves us. Unlearning one's privileged discourse so that, in fact, one can be heard by people who are not
within the academy is very different from clamoring for anti-intellectualism, a sort of complete monosyllabification of one's vocabulary within
academic enclosures. And it seems to me that one's practice is very
dependent upon one's positionality, one's situation. I come from a state
where the illiterate—not the functionally illiterate, but the real illiterate,
who can't tell the difference between one letter and another—are still
possessed of a great deal of political sophistication, and are certainly
not against learning a few things. I'm constantly struck by the anti-
intellectualism within the most opulent university systems in the world.
So that's where I was speaking about de-skilling.

WA   But the heart of my question nonetheless remains, and that is,
ought one to choose one's texts in the light of the interests, desires,
prejudgments of marginalized groups? Or ought one to choose one's
texts in light of what we suppose they ought to be interested in? Or
should there be no conscious choosing of texts of this type at all?

GS   Again, I don't know. I can only speak of my working life, which
has been spent as a teacher of literature in the United States, in Europe
and in England. It seems to me that I cannot speak of what marginalized
people ought to be interested in. In Melbourne I ended my talk with an
account of the suicide of a teenage woman in Calcutta in 1926. What I
was doing with the young woman who had killed herself was really
trying to analyze and represent her text. She wasn't particularly trying
to speak to me. I was representing her, I was reinscribing her. To an
extent, I was writing her to be read, and I certainly was not claiming to
give her a voice. So if I'm read as giving her a voice, there again this is
a sort of transaction of the positionality between the Western feminist
listener who listens to me, and myself, signified as a Third World informant. What we do toward the texts of the oppressed is very much
dependent upon where we are.

WA   Let me ask you one final question. In one of your talks in Melbourne, you said that the prime task of feminism should not be to retrace
the figure of woman. What did you mean by that?

GS   Well, I was trying to say that although Derrida was, in some
ways, retracing the figure of woman, that's not identical with the project
of feminism. And I was really talking about "global feminism", since that
seems always to be on the agenda these days when one speaks in the
West. It seems to me that if one's talking about the prime task, since

there is no discursive continuity among women, the prime task is situational anti-sexism, and the recognition of the heterogenity of the field, instead of positing some kind of woman's subject, women's figure, that kind of stuff. It seems to me, if you really want to trace the figure, then you should start looking elsewhere in the globe. Psychoanalysis and counterpsychoanalysis can easily become the gift of capitalist imperialism to the cause of feminism.

WA   So you're saying that tracing the figure of woman would be another one of those essentialisms which you think it is better to avoid.

GS   In the name of anti-essentialism, and in the hands of hegemonic feminists, it sometimes becomes that. If one can situate it geopolitically, if one can situate it within the work place, I think some excellent work can be done, is being done, and tracing what we are calling the figure of woman. But when we speak of the "prime task", my heart is elsewhere.

5

Questions of Multi-culturalism

This discussion between Sneja Gunew and Gayatri Spivak concerning the post-colonialism, anti-imperialism and multi-cultural politics in Australia was first published in Hecate: An Interdisciplinary Journal of Women's Liberation, *Vol. 12, No. 1/2, 1986. The interview also appeared in* Women's Writing in Exile, *edited by Mary Lynn Broe and Angela Ingram (Chapel Hill: UCP, 1989). This interview as originally broadcast on ABC Radio National on Saturday, August 30, 1986, in "The Minders" series, produced by Penny O'Donnell and Ed Brunetti.*

SG   We might begin with the whole notion of authenticity—a question that keeps coming up in relation to the kind of writing that I am publicising at the moment. I now refer to it as non-Anglo-Celtic rather than Migrant writing, since within Australia, Migrant connotes an inability to speak English. Thus, it is the writing of non-Anglo-Celts but in English. The question that keeps arising in relation to this is the question of authenticity. And it takes various forms, but I suppose one way of, in a sense, caricaturing it but, also, making it accessible is: "Aren't Patrick White's Middle Europeans or Beverley Farmer's Greeks just as authentic as the Greeks created by πO's poetry or by Antigone Kefala?" In a sense, putting the question this way covers over, or makes invisible, other forms, other questions that could be posed, such as: "But why do these Anglo-Celts have access to publishing, to writing, to be part of Australian literature, and why are other writers like Kefala, Ania Walwicz, Rosa Cappiello, etc., not seen as part of these cultural productions, why aren't they given a full measure of cultural franchise? In fact, in some senses, far from being invisible, the Migrant has always been constructed within Australian discursive formations, not just literature; and in literary forms the first such construction was Nino Culotta, who was an Irish journalist posing as an Italian, and wrote the most famous book for many, many decades about being an Italian immigrant trying to make it in Australia. And this book, I remember, was given to numerous immigrants as they arrived in Australia as some kind of explication of their status within the community, and is quite horrendous in all sorts of ways.

GCS   For me, the question 'Who should speak?' is less crucial than 'Who will listen?' 'I will speak for myself as a Third World person' is an important position for political mobilization today. But the real demand is that, when I speak from that position, I should be listened to seriously; not with that kind of benevolent imperialism, really, which simply says that because I happen to be an Indian or whatever . . . A hundred years ago it was impossible for me to speak , for the precise reason that makes it only too possible for me to speak in certain circles now. I see in that a kind of reversal, which is again a little suspicious. On the other hand, it is very important to hold on to it as a slogan in our time. The question of 'speaking *as*' involves a distancing from oneself. The moment I have to think of the ways in which I will speak as an Indian, or as a feminist, the ways in which I will speak as a woman, what I am doing is trying to generalise myself, make myself a representative, trying to distance myself from some kind of inchoate speaking *as such*. There are many subject positions which one must inhabit; one is not just one thing. That is when a political consciousness comes in. So that in fact, for the person who does the 'speaking as' something, it is a problem of distancing from one's self, whatever that self might be. But when the cardcarrying listeners, the hegemonic people, the dominant people, talk about listening to someone 'speaking as' something or the other, I think *there* one encounters a problem. When *they* want to hear an Indian speaking as an Indian, a Third World woman speaking as a Third World woman, they cover over the fact of the ignorance that they are allowed to possess, into a kind of homogenization.

SG   Yes, and they choose what parts they want to hear, and they choose what they then do with this material; and what seems to happen in very crude ways, within the context of multiculturalism, is that certain people are elevated very quickly to those who speak for *all* immigrants: in terms of funding, and in terms of the dissemination of their work, etc. As a result, you don't hear about the rest, because "we have covered that", and those few token figures function as a very secure alibi. If you look at the proportion of, for example, multicultural, non-Anglo-Celtic artists who get funded by the Australian Council, they are a very small percentage, and often the same ones every year. Because it is, in fact, an incredible job to educate oneself to know just what is in the field, and who else is doing things. It requires a lot of labour; it is so much easier to have these recurrent token figures.

GCS   Proust in *A la recherche*, when someone is criticizing Françoise's French, writes "What is French but bad Latin?" So from that point of view, one can't distinguish, you can't say that it is a French position or a Roman position. This is what he is pointing at—the moment you say, "This is a white position", again you are homogenizing. I think there is safety in specificity rather than in those labels.

SG   This is what I was trying to refer to earlier when I was saying the question usually gets posed in the ways of asking: "Yes, but aren't Patrick White's Middle Europeans authentic?" That is not the issue, because the whole *notion* of authenticity, of the authentic migrant experience, is one that comes to us constructed by hegemonic voices; and so, what one has to tease out is what is *not* there. One way of doing this (if one has knowledge from a particular culture), is to say: But look, this is what is left out, this is what is covered over; this kind of construction is taking place, this kind of reading is being privileged or, these series of readings are being privileged; and then to ask, What readings are not privileged, what is not there, what questions can't be asked?

GCS   Subordinate people use this also; and we are not without a sense of irony: we use it. I talk a lot, right? And when I get very excited I interrupt people; and I am making a joke, but in fact it is never perceived as a joke unless I tell them. I will quite often say, "You know, in my culture it shows interest and respect if someone interrupts": and immediately there are these very pious faces, and people allow me to interrupt. It is not as if we don't perceive the homogenization; we exploit it, why not?

SG   So that what you have as one of the strategies of some of the writers that I work with, is that they play a kind of stage Migrant and poke fun at, and parody in all sorts of ways, these so-called authentic Migrant constructions. I am thinking here of the work of πO, the work of Ania Walwicz . . .

GCS   In fact, tokenization goes with ghettoization. These days, I am constantly invited to things so that I will present the Third World point of view; when you are perceived as a token, you are also silenced in a certain way because, as you say, if you have been brought there it has been covered, they needn't worry about it anymore, you salve their conscience. In the United States, being an Indian also brings a certain very curious problem. Over the centuries we have had histories of, let's say, Indian indentured labour being taken to the Afro-Caribbean. After the change of regimes in certain African nations, Indians moved from Africa, then to Britain; then Indians in waves in the early '60's, professional Indians, went to the United States as part of the brain drain. These Indians who are spread out over the world, for different kinds of historical reasons, they are diasporic . . .

SG   You could multiply this by the Greeks and the Italians in Australia, and numerous other ethnic groups who, for various reasons, have had to leave their original countries and move to other ones.

GCS   The Indian community in the United States is the only coloured community which came in with the brain drain. This is quite different from Indians and Pakistanis in Britain, and certainly very different from Indians of the Afro-Caribbean diaspora. And therefore we are used as an alibi, since we don't share the same history of oppression with the local Blacks, the east Asians, and the Hispanics; on the other hand, our skins are not white, and since most of us are post-colonials we were trained in the British way, so there is a certain sort of Anglomania in the United States, we can be used as affirmative-action alibis.

SG Yes, this happens to some extent, too, with Jewish immigrants, often refugees, who came at various stages to Australia. They too, are used in that sort of sense of affirmative action. For all sorts of reasons they have, some of them, come to very prominent positions and so they can be wheeled in very easily to say: "Of course, this is not an Anglo establishment, a predominantly Anglo establishment—we've got x, y, z." So a similar kind of alibi operates. One of the things, though, that I wanted to hear you talk about more was a notion you brought up yesterday, about this idea of earning the right to criticize. As I understand it, this can be a trap that is provided by a certain kind of privilege that comes with being this sort of token who is constantly brought in. I wonder if you could say more about that.

GCS It is a problem that is very close to my heart because I teach, after all, abroad. I will have in an undergraduate class, let's say, a young, white male student, politically-correct, who will say: "I am only a bourgeois white male, I can't speak." In that situation—it's peculiar, because I am in the position of power and their teacher and, on the other hand, I am not a bourgeois white male—I say to them: "Why not develop a certain degree of rage against the history that has written such an abject script for you that you are silenced?" Then you begin to investigate what it is that silences you, rather than take this very deterministic position— since my skin colour is this, since my sex is this, I cannot speak. I call these things, as you know, somewhat derisively, chromatism: basing everything on skin color—"I am white, I can't speak"—and genitalism: depending on what kind of genitals you have, you can or cannot speak in certain situations. From this position, then, I say you will of course not speak in the same way about the Third World material, but if you make it your task not only to learn what is going on there through language, through specific programmes of study, but also at the same time through a *historical* critique of your position as the investigating person, then you will see that you have earned the right to criticize, and you be heard. When you take the position of not doing your homework— "I will not criticize because of my accident of birth, the historical accident"—that is a much more pernicious position. In one way you take a risk to criticize, of criticizing something which is *Other*—something which you used to dominate. I say that you have to take a certain risk: to say

"I won't criticize" is salving your conscience, and allowing you not to do any homework. On the other hand, if you criticize having earned the right to do so, then you are indeed taking a risk and you will probably be made welcome, and can hope to be judged with respect.

SG   Perhaps the other side of the dilemma, though, is the sort of trap that people who are wheeled in as token figures speaking for those marginalized groups can fall into, where they deny their own privileged position. You were saying earlier, for example, that in a classroom situation you are the one with the power *vis-à-vis* the white Anglo-Saxon student. Similarly, I think that one forgets when one speaks within very obviously privileged academic contexts about, say, immigrant groups within Australia, that one is also very much in danger of homogenizing, and of misrepresenting, and of not really following through those questions carefully enough; distinguishing carefully enough between those differences that one speaks 'in the name of'. That business of speaking 'in the name of' is something about which I have a real phobia, and it is very difficult to think up strategies for undermining that.

GCS   And I don't think, really, that we will solve the problem today talking to each other; but, on the other hand, I think it has to be kept alive as a problem. It is not a solution, the idea of the disenfranchised speaking for themselves, or the radical critics speaking for them; this question of representation, self-representation, representing others, is a problem. On the other hand, we cannot put it under the carpet with demands for authentic voices; we have to remind ourselves that, as we do this, we might be compounding the problem even as we are trying to solve it. And there has to be a persistent critique of what one is up to, so that it doesn't get all bogged down in this homogenization; constructing the Other simply as an object of knowledge, leaving out the real Others because of the ones who are getting access into public places due to these waves of benevolence and so on. I think as long as one remains aware that it is a very problematic field, there is some hope.

SG   Yes, and one of the strategies that one has learnt from the Women's Movement, for example, is to make sure that you are constantly involved in political campaigns, that you are in touch with what is happening, that you are in touch with the very specific politics of trying to bring about certain reforms. So in a similar way, I suppose, one of the ways in the area of multiculturalism is to be very alert to what is happening with the various immigrant groups in terms of cultural politics. The kinds of things that are going on, the kinds of questions that are not being asked, what people are doing that has never been heard or seen— these are the sorts of issues.

GCS   Can you give some specific examples of problems of cultural politics in the Australian context?

SG   Well, for example, I was walking along Glebe Road, last week, and looked in a shop window and suddenly saw, amongst the clothing (this was a tailor's shop), a poem hanging there. And I walked in, and found a wonderful friend of mine, Nihat Ziyalan, who is a Turkish poet; and this is his way—one of the few ways that he can get heard—of making his work accessible to whoever is passing by. And people do apparently come in and talk to him about his work; but he certainly is not receiving any funding at the moment. Always there is this sense of voices in the wilderness, that are never going to get heard, not through the regular channels, be it the Australia Council, be it SBS. In the case of the latter, the ethnic broadcasting television station which is supposed to be serving multiculturalist Australia, in reality they get most of their programmes from overseas, so it is Europe imported back into Australia, rather than seeing certain kinds of European or Asian or Middle Eastern groups within Australia and latching into those.

GCS   This is the real problem, isn't it? We are back to some extent to where we started, the way in which one actually keeps talking about the same old things, that is to say: rather than look at the real problem of imperialism, to make it identical with the problems of immigrants; rather than look at the Third World at large, to make everything identical with the problem at home. This is, in fact, simply the old attitudes disguised in one way or another. This is the real difficulty with cultural politics. If you go, as I do, to African Literature Association conventions, what you notice is that the Black Americans—of course, when I generalize like this there are always notable exceptions—Black Americans are much more interested in the question of any Black tradition, whereas the Continental Africans are much more interested in the problems that they and their colleagues are making for themselves, in the problems of the various African nations, in the problems existing between European language productions in Africa, and what is happening to African languages as it's all getting organized into philosophy, the discipline of literature, and so on and so forth. What you really mark, is that it is the ones with United States passports who are trying to identify the problem of racism in the United States with what is happening in decolonized Africa.

SG   So again, that's the question of homogenization and that refusal of specificity.

GCS   Yes.

SG   And I think another thing that you have been referring to, that notion of a diaspora, that the diasporic cultures are quite different from the culture that they came from originally, and that sort of distinction—an elementary distinction, and also one, of course, that history teaches us is not made, and needs to be made.

GCS   You see these differences, in fact you feel them in the details of your daily life, because actually the system is not so blind—it's the benevolent ones who become blind in this way. I'll tell you a little story. I was at the Commonwealth Institute in London in March, to discuss some films made by Black Independent Film-makers in London (a wonderful group of people, I was very pleased they asked me), and one of the points I made to them was in fact (I am a bit of a broken record on this issue). "You are diasporic Blacks in Britain, and you are connecting to the local lines of resistance in Britain, and you are therefore able to produce a certain kind of idiom of resistance; but don't forget the Third World at large, where you won't be able to dissolve everything into Black against White, as there is also Black against Black, Brown against Brown, and so on." These young men and women thought I was asking them to connect with some kind of mystical ethnic origin because, of course, when they were brought into the places which they inhabit, their sense of the old country was from the nostalgic longing towards customs, cooking, and so on and so forth, that they saw in their families. And so they were rebelling against what is basically a generational problem, and transforming it into a total ignoring of what is going on in the Third World at large. On the other hand, the system knows I am a resident alien in the United States; at that point I was actually lecturing in Canada, at the University of Alberta. I crossed from upstate New York into Toronto (I carry an Indian passport) with no problem because, of course, and Indian resident in the United States would not, the thinking goes, want to become an illegal immigrant in Canada. Two days later, I went to London, I did my programme, and was returning back to Canada with the same passport, same resident alien's visa in the United States, and I was supposed to take a plane from Heathrow on Sunday. Air Canada says to me: "We can't accept you." I said: "Why?" and she said: "You need a visa to go to Canada." I said: "Look here, I am the same person, the same passport . . . " Indian cultural identity, right? but you become different. When it is from London, Indians can very well want to jump ship to Canada; I need a visa to travel from London to Canada on the same passport, but not from the United States. To cut a long story short, I was talking about a related problem to the Black men and women who had made the films, and then it happened in my own life. In the end, I had to stay another day, and telephone Canada and tell them that I could not give my seminar. I said to the woman finally before I left, in some bitterness: "Just let me tell you one small thing: Don't say 'We can't accept you', that sounds very bad from one human being to another; next time you should say: 'The regulations are against it'; then we are both victims." And the woman looked at me with such astonishment because, in Heathrow, a coloured woman wearing a sari does not speak to a white woman like this. There, I was indeed speaking as an Indian, in that particular situation. So in those kinds of things, once you begin to look at the way regulations work, you will see the differences *are* made among different kinds of Third World peoples—but not when one is being benevolent.

SG   What is very much a question for me at the moment is that if you are constructed in one particular kind of language, what kinds of violence does it do to your subjectivity if one then has to move into another language, and suppress whatever selves or subjectivities were constructed by the first? And of course, some people have to pass through this process several times. And a small gesture towards beginning to understand this would be to create a demand for multi-lingual anthologies within Australia. These is an incredible and disproportionate resistance to presenting the general Australian public with immigrant writing *in English* even, but to have it in conjunction with the remainder of these repressed languages seems to be another battle which still has to be fought.

GCS   One hears, for example, that some of the theoretical stuff that's produced, let's say, in France, is naturally accessible to people from Africa, from India, from these so-called natural places. If one looks at the history of post-Enlightenment theory, the major problem has been the problem of autobiography: how subjective structures can, in fact, give objective truth. During these same centuries, the Native Informant, who was found in these other places, his stuff was unquestioningly treated as the objective evidence for the founding of so-called sciences like ethnography, ethno-linguistics, comparative religion, and so on. So that, once again, the theoretical problems only relate to the person who knows. The person who *knows* has all of the problems of selfhood. The person who is *known*, somehow seems not to have a problematic self. These days, it is the same kind of agenda that is at work. Only the dominant self can be problematic; the self of the Other is authentic without a problem, naturally available to all kinds of complications. This is very frightening.

6

The Post-colonial Critic

*In 1987, Gayatri Spivak held a visiting profes-
sorship at the Centre for Historical Studies at
Jawaharlal Nehru University, New Delhi, where
she offered a course entitled "Texts and Contexts:
Theories of Interpretation," which focused on recent post-structuralist European theories, chiefly
those of Derrida, Foucault, Lyotard, Baudrillard, Habermas and Lacan. She also delivered
several lectures at various centres in Delhi University. Rashmi Bhatnagar, Lola Chatterjee and
Rajeshwari Sunder Rajan focused their interview
with Gayatri Spivak on four broad areas: the
situation of the post-colonial intellectual, first
world theory, the women's movement and the
study of English literature. First published in*
The Book Review, *Vol. 11, No. 3, 1987.*

Q   There are several questions that arise out of the way you perceive
yourself ('The post-colonial diasporic Indian who seeks to decolonize
the mind'), and the way you constitute us (for convenience, 'native'
intellectuals):

a. Your commitment to rendering visible the historical and institutional structures from within which you speak explains your explo-
   ration of the diasporic condition of the post-colonial Indian academic in the US. What are the theories or explanations, the
   narratives of affiliation and disaffiliation that you bring to the politically contaminated and ambivalent function of the non-resident
   Indian (NRI) who comes back to India, however temporarily, upon
   the winds of progress?
b. Are you privileging exile as a vantage point for a clearer perspective
   on the scene of post-colonial cultural politics?
c. Would you say that your pedagogic practice here in the classroom,
   say at JNU, conveys the terms of your engagement with the Indian
   scene?

GCS   In the first place, your description of how I constitute you does
not seem quite correct. I thought I constituted you, equally with the
diasporic Indian, as a post-colonial intellectual!

As for how I came to be in Delhi, these were for reasons that were not sufficiently clear to me then, reasons that have more to do with an unexamined life than with exile. I'd like to say that an exile is some one who is obliged to stay away—I am not in that sense an exile.

The space I occupy might be explained by my history. It is a position into which I have been written. I am not privileging it, but I do want to use it. I can't fully construct a position that is different from the one I am in.

As for my engagement with the Indian scene, I don't think one can construct an engagement out of a visiting professorship!

And I am not sure why I am more 'politically contaminated' than you.

RB & RS   The sense in which we used the notion of contamination was not to suggest a degree of purity for ourselves. Perhaps the relationship of distance and proximity between you and us is that what we write and teach has political and other actual consequences for us that are in a sense different from the consequences, or lack of consequences, for you. In this context, how is it possible to work against the grain of one's space?

GCS   No one can quite articulate the space she herself inhabits. My attempt has been to describe this relatively ungraspable space in terms of what might be its history. I'm always uneasy if I'm asked to speak for my space—it's the thing that seems to be most problematic, and something that one really only learns from other people. I was really therefore most interested in your notion of the 'freedom' involved with being an NRI. One never quite understands this 'freedom'.

It's also difficult for me to make claims for working against the grain. In my second lecture at JNU, I specified my position only because I was asked to, and since then I have found myself foregrounding it rather more than I anticipated having to.

RB   I recall that in the essay 'French Feminism in an International Frame", you claimed for yourself only the negotiations operative for an 'academic feminist'—the crucial definition for you arising from the workplace.

GCS   I call myself an academic feminist so as to make my claim minimal. If one has to define oneself irreducibly, it must be in minimal terms.

Mine really has been a small effort to come to an understanding of these problems, and the effort has been influenced by the site of the university.

I really am here because I wanted to learn a little more about how objects of historical investigation are made when there is not enough evidence, and what consequences that has for cultural explanations. Being an Indian by birth and citizenship, I find that this inquiry and the terms of this inquiry somehow get articulated into a place from which I can speak to others. I have never travelled anywhere without a job because it seems to be one way of finding out what the problems with one's space might be, and of involving oneself in the place one visits.

It is my conviction that you probably understand the complexities of my space as diasporic Indian intellectual better than I can. That too is part of the instruction I want to receive.

LC   The NRI is defined here primarily in economic terms—the Indian abroad invests money in India because it is more profitable!

GCS   That kind of economic definition is closer to the point. I certainly have no money to invest here, and I don't fit in with the Indian community abroad. I like to think that the drunken father in 'My Beautiful Laundrette' offers a stereotype that is closest to the space I occupy. He uses an outdated 'socialist' language in a colonial accent while the actual NRIs are integrated into the chicaneries of local small capital.

Q   In the process of investigating 'the matter of the colonies' using First World elite theory, you have said that you use the resistance of the matter to theory as a way of opening up theory.

   a. Now there is a certain uneasiness here about the ideological contamination of theory by the specific historical origins which produce it and therefore about the implications of employing it in our own context. Would you defend the post-colonial intellectual dependence upon Western models as historical necessity?
   b. This question is inevitable: what are the possibilities of discovering/promoting indigenous theory?

GCS   I don't use only First World theory—I have intervened, for instance, in the debate on the use of Sanskrit (in my lectures on 'Didi', as well as 'Standayini'[2]). I believe in using what one has, and this has nothing to do with privileging First World theories. What is an indigenous theory?

RB   Well, that was the question. Take something like Gandhism, even though it is a highly synthesized model. . . .

GCS   I cannot understand what indigenous theory there might be that can ignore the reality of nineteenth-century history. As for syntheses: syntheses have more problems than answers to offer. To construct indigenous theories one must ignore the last few centuries of historical involvement. I would rather use what history has written for me.

I am not interested in defending the post-colonial intellectual's dependence on Western models: my work lies in making clear my disciplinary predicament. My position is generally a reactive one. I am viewed by the Marxists as too codic, by feminists as too male-identified, by indigenous theorists as too committed to Western theory. I am uneasily pleased about this. One's vigilance is sharpened by the way one is perceived, but it does not involve defending oneself.

Q   Why does your theory lever the woman question via homologies and analogies? Why is it necessary to have a series of discontinuous displacements of the concept—metaphors from, say, Marx's text to, say, a text of Mahasweta Devi's? Why is there a structure of postponements in your work which you have yourself noticed in Derrida and Foucault? So we have read and assented to your cautionary narratives for a readership of First World feminists.[3] What is it you now say to us?

GCS   I'm very glad that you gave me a sense of how you perceive the woman question in the hierarchy of my theory. I think this structure of postponements that you have noticed relates to what I've been saying in the classroom. I see my charge as teaching post-structuralist theory.

My own feeling is that the constituency of feminism is one that even when I work with feminists and for them, it is inevitably from above. I perceive that constituency as my judges. However even as I acknowledge their judgement, I can't accept their judgement to the extent of changing myself in response to it. When I speak about my position, I really speak only to women like you who are, by my understanding, in as much of the predicament of the post-colonial intellectual as I am.

This is one of the reasons why I seem to be working within a structure of postponements. I think the hardest lesson for me to learn—and I have not learnt it, one attempts to learn it everyday—is that the word 'woman' is not after all something for which one can find a literal referent without looking into the looking glass. And as you have yourself realized, what I see in the looking glass is not particularly the constituency of feminism. In a situation like that I think one has to postpone indefinitely even as one constantly indicates possibilities of connections and practice. And I am afraid of speaking too quickly in academic situations about the women—the tribal subaltern, the urban sub-proletariat, the unorganized peasant—to whom I have not learnt to make myself acceptable other than as a concerned benevolent person who is free to come and go. And this is a condition which you share with me. I find that to be a much more difficult problem to work at than all of the differences between living abroad and living at home.

As far as my theoretical interventions go—I don't want to be confessional or autobiographical—but all my invited lectures here[4] were about women (perhaps not woman). I have, for instance, tried to write about the loneliness of the gendered woman in Mahasweta Devi's Stanadayini, about how unexpectedly and singularly the other woman is located in her 'Hunter', and offered an examination of our own production as emancipated female readers in my discussion of Tagore's 'Didi'.

Q   The regulative psychobiography for Indian women, according to you, is sanctioned suicide.[5] Now the notion of alternative psychobiographies—alternative to the Freudian family romance—is an attractive and powerful idea and not just for academic mileage, but in the arena of Indian women's cultural self representations.

But is there a danger in sanctioned suicide being the regulative psychobiography, that there are other realities and other myths that you will overlook? Is there a danger in sanctioned suicide becoming the master key, and of regulative psychobiography becoming prey to a kind of negativeness?

GCS   When I began to discover the argument of sanctioned suicide, what I was trying to do was to find an alternative regulative psychobiography at work outside of both psychoanalysis and counterpsychoanalysis. Of course sanctioned suicide is not a master key, and of course it can become dangerously starting, but that was for me only a diagnostic point.

Q   Would you like to discuss the pragmatic political usefulness of your own recent work which has focussed on the subaltern gendered subject?

GCS   I cannot get a hold on what is meant by a direct pragmatic political usefulness which might be unrelated to the classroom. In America some people say their pedagogy is their politics—I think it can be a kind of alibi. In the long run, and I am sorry if I seem too reactive here, I would like to learn about the political usefulness of my work, whatever it might be, from the outside, and from an outside which I inhabit myself. If you ask me directly what its pragmatic political usefulness is, I would say very little . . . as little as anyone else's.

Q   In terms of reading critical procedures you recommended, in your lecture on 'The Burden of English Studies in the Colonies', negotiating with the structures of violence. This produced at once a level of assert and a number of problems that we put to you in very naive fashion: how does one negotiate from a position which some of us English teachers often see as a position of political impotence, cultural irrelevance, ideological distortion—our only power being the power of the hegemonic, Western-educated liberalism that inhabits us? Furthermore, is there in your notion of 'negotiation' something of the rarefied and oversubtle which may emanate from the complexities of your own position as diasporic intellectual, and which we would buy at our cost since our realities surely need connotations of a stronger and more formal intervention? Would you like to elaborate the theory of negotiation in the face of such unease and such interest?

GCS   Well, if it is rarefied and oversubtle, you would know how better than I.

As far as I can understand, in order to intervene one must negotiate. If there is anything I have learnt in and through the last 23 years of teaching, it is that the more vulnerable your position, the more you have to negotiate. We are not talking about discursive negotiations, or negotiation between equals, not even a collective bargaining. It seems to me that if you are in a position where you are, as you have said, being constituted by Western liberalism, you have to negotiate to see what positive role you can play from within the constraints of western liberalism (which is a very broad term) breaking it open. I am not sure what formal intervention in your question might mean. If you mean that you have to make interventions in the structure of which you are part, it seems to me that is the most negotiated position, because you must intervene even as you inhabit those structures.

Since I really don't understand what the oversubtlety of it is I guess all I mean by negotiation here is that one tries to change something that one is obliged to inhabit, since one is not working from the outside. In order to keep one's effectiveness, one must also preserve those structures—not cut them down completely. And that, as far as I can understand, is negotiation. You inhabit the structures of violence and violation, here defined by you as Western liberalism.

Here again, I don't think the difference is between rarefaction and super subtlety on one side, and the need for stronger interventions on the other. Once again I would look at the ethico-political agenda that creates such a differentiation, such as defining of one's self.

I notice in your questions a kind of warning which, pared down to the essentials, is: don't talk at us, you are in a different position. I would think again, since this is the kind of thing I meditate on, of what the other person defines me as in order to define herself. You might want to think and mediate on your own desires in that matter.

RS Instead of the solipsism of meditation, is it possible to achieve a dialogue, an exchange? I think the attempt has been from our side to communicate to you something of our conditions of work.

GCS Since we have been talking about elite theory, let me suggest that, that is the kind of position Jurgen Habermas articulates: a neutral communication situation of free dialogue. Well, it is not a situation that ever comes into being—there is no such thing. The desire for neutrality and dialogue, even as it should not be repressed, must always mark its own failure. To see how desire articulates itself, one must read the text in which that desire is expressed. The idea of neutral dialogue is an idea which denies history, denies structure, denies the positioning of subjects. I would try to look how, in fact, the demand for a dialogue is articulated.

Q When you speak of the 'burden' of English studies, we recognise the double burden upon the third world woman teacher of English literature. Because of course this is her enclave and her privilege it is the 'suitable' profession, and the suitable undergraduate course for Indian women. So there are at many levels simulations of a gendered perspective—this even while the woman teacher of English negotiates, or hopes she negotiates, with the epistemic violence visited on her women students and on her own self in the family, in the workplace and on the street. How does all this translate into pedagogic practice? What kind of dialogue do we set up between the teaching of English and the women's movement here, so that reality is not outside the classroom?

GCS   The two areas you mention, English literature and the Women's Movement—are discontinuous, though not unrelated. They would bring each other to crisis.

The teaching of English literature, if one looks at its definition, has very little involvement with the Women's Movement—not just in India, but elsewhere too. Literature occupies a kind of enchanted space within intellectual history since at least the end of the eighteenth century in Europe.

In terms of teaching English (not in terms of the Women's Movement), I think that what I have been trying to do in my small way is to show how they—the makers of English literature—need us.

For example, the place of widow sacrifice in Jane Eyre as an unacknowledged metaphor leads to an extremely odd reading of the novel.[6] But I wanted to push that odd reading, since it shows how the English nineteenth century needed the axiomatics of imperialism in order to construct itself. I think that is about all we can do within the pedagogy of English literature.

I also try to look at the subject position of the colonial intellectual within texts produced in the colonies at the same time as British or French texts: so I try to teach Kim and Gora at the same time. I am not supporting either—there is no dialogue between the two, and they are both constructed out of situations of power, and constructed differently. I think these are the two things, with my limited training, that I can do in the English literature classroom: to see how the master texts need us in the construction of their texts without acknowledging that need; and to explore the differences and similarities between texts coming from the two sides which are engaged with the same problem at the same time. The connection between this and the Women's Movement is discontinuous, though not unrelated, as I said, and each brings the other to crisis.

Notes

1. Yale French Studies: Feminist Readings, French Texts/American Contexts, No. 62, 1981.

2."The Burden of English Studies in the Colonies: Tagore's Didi" the V. Krishna Memorial Lecture delivered at Miranda House, Delhi University, in February 1987. Paper on Mahasweta Devi's Stanadyini' read at a symposium, constructing women held at the Department of Sociology, Delhi University, in February 1987.

3. "Draupadi': by Mahasweta Devi in *Writing and Sexual Difference*, ed. Elizabeth Alsel (Chicago: University of Chicago Press, 1982).

4. See (3) above. Also lecture on Mahasweta Devi's 'The Hunter' delivered to the Comparative Literature Association, Delhi University, in March 1987.

5. "Can the Subaltern Speak? Speculations on Widow Sacrifice", Wedge 7/8, Winter/ Spring, 1985.

6. "Three Women's Texts and a Critique of Imperialism" Critical Inquiry 12, Autumn 1985.

7

Postmarked Calcutta, India

*This discussion concerning the problems of representa-
tion, self-representation and representing others, and
the situation of the post-colonial subject between Angela
Ingram and Gayatri Spivak was recorded in November,
1987, upon Gayatri Spivak's return from her visiting
professorship at the Centre for Historical Studies at Jawaharlal Nehru University, New Delhi.*

GCS   Yes. I'd never taught in India and I discovered a lot of things.
Before I went I'd chanced upon a book by a white U.S. male, *Mortal
Questions* by Thomas Nagel. It said something which really gave me a
kind of understanding about what was happening to me in India, after
the event. Talking about his feeling during the Vietnam years that his
theoretical preoccupations—he is a philosopher—were absurd, he writes
"Citizenship is a difficult burden, especially for those of us who are not
very patriotic." You see? I am an unpatriotic citizen of India. I have never
taught anywhere where I would feel the special burden Nagel is writing
about. This whole business of speaking *as* something, well, this is a *big*
thing: speaking as a citizen. I never had. Citizenship is such an abstract
concept. But this is the fortieth year of Indian independence, you know,
1947. I kept thinking over and over again that independence in decolonization was really the possibility of citizenship. However abstract the
notion is, there is some kind of a thing about the people that you're
speaking to having the same kinds of political choices within the system
of government, even of breaking the rules. That's the thing that really
made me feel very strange.

A   That occurred to me when I read the *Hecate* piece and you said,
sort of parenthetically, "I carry an Indian passport". Did you never think
to take American whatever it's called. . .

GCS   Citizenship! Well, you know, at first it was really sentimentality.
I came in '61; it was in '66 that I got my green card.

A   That took a long time. Did you come as a student?

GCS   I came as a student, so I hadn't really thought of getting a green
card. I had married a man, a white United States male, and I did not feel

like subsuming my identity under his. And I guess I also had at that point a feeling that I did not want to be an American. It was not because I didn't know that I was going to stay for as long as I have. It was not wanting to be an Indian, because to an extent my first convictions were those of an internationalist. Although I think internationalism is one of those unifying alibis for decolonization, it is still a strategy I admire or appreciate. It's the kind of strategy where without destroying these ideas one also shows that they have historical fault lines, you know, secularism, nationalism, internationalism, culturalism. If one sees how these things develop historically and how it's tied up with the hegemony of, basically, Western Europe, one can see that it's not that the ideas are bad, but that the ideas are vulnerable, and the ideas are especially vulnerable if they're thought of as transcendental or universal. As a decolonized citizen you take a distance from them; you don't throw them away. So it wasn't that I particularly wanted to remain an *Indian*, I really felt that I did not want to be identified with the superpower. Having been a British subject, I did not want to become a U.S. citizen, move, like the British Empire, from territorial imperialism to neo-colonialism [I'm now quoting Karl Pletsch], "the British Empire passing into the hands of the United States." Even at that early stage I did not want actually to trace that itinerary in my own life. I think that's really what it was. In my conversation with Sneja [see chapter 5], didn't you feel that it gave me a certain kind of position from which to speak?

A   Yes. And I wondered about it. I told you I have a German friend who's taken American citizenship, and that she and I always agree, rather shamefacedly, that we know that being aliens (I'm a resident alien; it says so on the card—

GCS   That's what I am, too—)

A   —being that—and one's ashamed of it—is being in a position one can exploit. It gives one a certain something or another. But we're both white, and that's one of the things that, obviously, makes an enormous difference.

Anyway, yes, "a position from which to speak": where do you speak from in India, where you had never taught and seeing that you've been here being famous for these many moons, being whatever you are here? What was it like, in other words?

GCS   You see—it's kind of you to say I'm famous—there are in my group lots of people who have made good abroad.

A   What do you mean, your group? Which group?

GCS   You know, my generation, as it were.

A   Of Indians?

GCS   Yes.

A   I meant in your "field", whatever that was when I met you. You were being "a Derridean", a very famous name in that critical group.

GCS   I'll tell you what is. If I could just backtrack because you said something very interesting before, I'll remember this question and I'll go on with it. I think one of the things I was trying to say in my conversation with Sneja, I really felt even *more* strongly teaching in India, that it isn't necessarily bad being white, because to an extent it is what one *does* with the fact that one's white at this point that's more important, isn't it? And one of the things about British colonialism in India is that at no stage was there a very large number of British in India. How was it that they were so successful in establishing and imposing that kind of repressive structured government? Because—and I am not the only one who says this—in fact the indigenous elite found that wonderful structure of repression a structure that they could identify with and could use to actually entrench their own position. And as a sort of by-product, what happened was what I have called elsewhere epistemic violence and the production of the colonial subject. *That* thing I felt even more strongly, the detritus of all that. (I was teaching in the capital city.) So that one really senses that yes, if a resident alien's white, she's not necessarily good, but she's not necessarily bad, either. It's this sense, I think, that was developed more.

Now I'll come back to your question. What is interesting is I went to India to teach. I was asked to teach. Now where I was teaching, the Modern Language people would not have me. Not everyone, sorry, but there was very strong resistance because there was a feeling that I wasn't really French enough to be speaking for all these French intellectuals and I was "from the United States". So there were (talking of indigenous elites) indigenous teachers who were more French than I was. It wasn't that I wasn't Indian enough. (I taught at the Centre for Historical Studies, at a very elite university.) What had I been asked to talk about? Recent theories of interpretation—by which was meant Foucault, Derrida, postmodernism, and how they related to historiography. I felt very much that this was the sort of "information retrieval" situation which is the exact legitimizing counterpart of what happens here when I am asked to speak as a "Third World" woman.

Once I began, however, I was confronted by people who wanted me to prove that I was in fact not a sort of anti-Indian racist. Mind you, I was asked to teach all this stuff, but I had to prove at the same time that I was also an authentic Indian, and a real Marxist.

A   And still there were places that thought they had indigenous Indian people who were more French than you?

GCS   Yes.

A   And the "taint" was that you'd been in America, rather than in France?

GCS   Yes, because there is still, among the elite, a very strong colonial identification with European traditions of thinking, rather than U.S., so the real problem was much more that I was coming from *that* country rather than the old masters. But then I went to Calcutta, my home town, where I had been asked to teach the Critique of Humanism and so on, and I must say that I had a better time there because I knew the people who had asked me and their production was almost exactly the same: in other words, same class, same college, same prejudices, and so on. That was a pleasure.

A   But they hadn't been in America?

GCS   Well, one of them had been to Rochester for a Ph.D. I mean, there wasn't that feeling of "You're not British", if you know what I mean. But then when I would speak about Third Worldism, and how in Western Third Worldism there was a collaboration with the Third World intellectuals who were producing a "Third World", what I would get back is, "Well, how about domestic First Worldism, which is why you're here." (!)
So I started talking a great deal about the post-colonial diasporic—if you'll allow me to use the word. You're right in saying that the diasporic really is not someone who chooses to exile herself.

A   No, I don't *know* about that. It's just that the word has come up in conversations with other people and I wonder about it.

GCS   I'm not absolutely sure. But I began to speak much more, and I really began to *look* much more at what was happening to the people who lived abroad, however much they despised the United States. It was in fact the term that I used this afternoon [November 6, 1987, at the University of Texas, Austin]; it's a term that is used by the government of India, the "non-resident Indian". You're a resident alien here. I'm not a real NRI because my passport is Indian. But the non-resident Indians who're really made welcome and given breaks, investment breaks and so on, are the U.S. Indians. So I began to look at what, in spite of all of these attitudes, it was that was being privileged in the country. And that's what really became much clearer to me, the position of the First World Indian diasporic, especially in the United States, which is very different from Indians elsewhere.

A   That's another thing I was going to ask you. It's absolutely unique, is it? In America?

GCS   Well, it's never "absolutely unique" anywhere. Someone always stands up and says, "Look here, what about this?"

A   Well, I thought, Australia? I thought, don't be so stupid; that's part of "the Commonwealth".

GCS   Right.

A   Then I thought Canada.

GCS   No! No way! How about the story that I tell at the end of my conversation [with Sneja].

A   But that was about your coming back to Canada, so it was the English treating you in that way.

GCS   No. Not at all.

A   It was the Canadians?

GCS   It was the Canadians. It's not the same as a class anywhere else.

A   And is it because you talk with an English accent?

GCS   No. It's because I am an Indian who lives in the United States. The passport tells you. The green card, the resident alien card.

A   Yes, but in the *Hecate* piece you said something about "Anglomania": "And therefore we are used as an alibi, since we don't share the same history of oppression with the local Blacks, the East Asians, and the Hispanics; on the other hand, our skins are not white, and since most of us are post-colonials we were trained in the British way, so there is a certain sort of Anglomania in the United States also, we can be used as affirmative-action alibis." Well, you were trained "in the British way", but you're not white. I heard a terrible story about a national women's conference a few years ago. An Indian woman had come all the way from India (perhaps not only for that, but she certainly wasn't someone who lived in this country). She had to register and, as far as I remember, the only categories were "white" and "Black" and "Hispanic", and she didn't know what to do. Perhaps there was "Other".

GCS   "Other" is what I always register as.

A   So she said "other" and was accused of "denying her ethnicity", and told she should have put herself down as "Black".

GCS   Well, in Britain, of course, it would make sense. But you know that's not what I meant. I meant that this is not a question of Anglomania in the United States. That was just a side thing. It's that Canada is more likely to be, for the Indian person from Britain or India, a place where he or she might want to become an illegal alien. Whereas the Indian person who resides in the United States is not going to want to become an illegal alien in *Canada*. The same passport—namely, the Indian passport—requires a visa to enter Canada if that person is coming from Britain, whereas it doesn't if that person is coming from the United States. It's the same person, same passport, but the visa regulations are different.

A   And I assume you carry the damn card with you all the time.

GCS   Yes.

A   Even though in England you say, "I'm an American resident, legal"?

GCS   No. It makes no difference, because they have to have some kind of . . . I mean, that would make it too obvious, wouldn't it?

Another thing I really felt being in India for this length of time was the difference in the women's movement. It involves itself much more with problem areas for women, and I must say that they also go beyond just problem areas for women. When it involves the kinds of problems other than the problems that a women's group might have or women as a gender might have, they go beyond that and tackle this stuff. But, in the very large majority of completely disenfranchised women in India, if a problem is not located, there is no sense of any contact with anything like feminist consciousness. And I was very much more interested in such persons—not as an observer, but in terms of wanting to connect, wanting and trying to really be their friend. It was a hard thing, you know. I'm trying not to talk about it in a very grand way at all. That's something that I felt very strongly about, the work, for example, that I, in a very minor way, do as sort of Mahasweta Devi's henchwoman with the tribals. You know, tribal women really are so much *not* within the circuit of the women's movement as such, that I think it is a very, very important experience that I had in India this time.

A   Are they partly not within the circuit because they're geographically isolated? Is that a factor?

GCS   No. It's just the women's problems that can be isolated: the bride-burning problem, for example, which is very much the Hindu, Muslim, Sikh working class, or the problem of organised labour—or unorganised labour that's definitely *not* within a union—that kind of a thing, or all the so-called semi-feudal problems related to the marriage structure. I'm not a great admirer of Foucault, but nonetheless, one really feels like agreeing that it's because the problems of the *tribal* woman are not immediately locatable as women's problems. Also, for the ones who are female without these locatable problems—since there is no circuit of socialised capital, there is no real circuit of commercials, advertisements, etc., developed to really hit them—they remain outside of the solutions.

It's almost as if you didn't qualify for these problems. You can remain satisfied within the patriarchal ideology, and it's all right, or you can be not that much within the patriarchal ideology, and that's all right, too. You're neither models nor problems.

A   You're just a long way away, over there.

GCS   Yes. And then, you know, they might not be geographically so very far from anything. That's why, I think, given that I'm a literary-type person, I'm very interested in them, and this is something that I said in the conversation [with Sneja] too, but I didn't quite have the tangible experience. Just wanting to do the old one-on-one. I don't want to produce any testimony literature, or oral histories, or witnessings from these women. I just want to see what happens and it's very, very hard.

Well, I tell you. You asked me am I a token in India. Yes. I'm a *mad* token in India. Loved it.

A   What are you a token of?

GCS   Well, the thing is, of course, when I say the word "India" we're using it as a metonym, right? I mean, we don't mean the 792 million people. I have just said that since it's not within the circuit of socialised capital, the India we are talking about is like Proust's Paris. It's very small. There is the same kind of academic provincialism in India as there is, let's say, in Britain or in Australia. That is to say, there are not too many universities; access to education is extremely class-fixed.

A   To that education, not to ordinary school education?

GCS   Well, even ordinary school education, but of course we are not talking about where I'm a token in terms of that. And yes, I'm a token of anything, you know. Just success. Just someone who can speak on Third-World feminism. Can you imagine the joke of being asked to speak on Third-World feminism in India? Someone who knows all these French theories. I don't know. I can't out my finger on it. But there is something.

A   At least when you walk into the airport in Delhi, you're absolutely unnoticeable.

GCS   Am I?

A   I would have thought so. Except for your hair, of course.

GCS   Height!

A   Well, you are very tall, and I was thinking about that, too. But you're a tall person and there must be other tall Indians around, tall Indian women. But about your hair. How many Indian women have their hair . . . spiked? How many Indian women of your age, "ordinary" Indian women, middle/upper class Indian women.

GCS   No one. No one. But you see, it's very complicated. Just as hair on legs in this country is a signifier of various sorts, it is in one way a signifier of a certain kind of 1960s feminist, right? Hair, as you must know, is an extremely important signifier in terms of femininity, so, like the hair on legs here, my hair is a signifier—of a widow's cut. Okay? So that if one doesn't know that this is supposed to be a fairly whatever-you-call-it kind of haircut here, people in fact commiserate because of course at forty-five I'm *way* beyond any kind of viable age for sexuality. I'm "childless", right? Of course I married in May, as you might know, but before that I also sort of gone through two "husbands" who were white anyway, so it was considered that I had agreed to accept my station in life. This wasn't seen as a spiked haircut, it was seen as a widow's cut. It wasn't recognised as a stylish Western cut.

A   You were just a poor widow lady. Who was very tall.

GCS   Yes. And also, funnily enough, I don't dress well, according to Indian terms. No, in fact I dress hopelessly. The only way (I mean, I can look strange), if I want to get "something done", I will produce an English which is *very* fake Britishy-sounding, and then I think I am considered some kind of foreign person who is *so* eccentric that she can dress like this. See, I've been asked in Calcutta where I learnt Bengali so well. Because I'm dressed so poorly.

A   Do they ever suggest where *they* think you come from?

GCS   Yes. And then I ask the question: "Where do you think I was made?"

A   Well, you could be a British Indian, I suppose, with two or three generations living in England behind you.

GCS   No. No woman speaks Bengali like me who is not in fact a Bengali. It's just that they're thrown off. I'm an anomaly. It's the whole cross-cultural business. I also found out how bicultural I was. Here, always, even when I'm wearing Western clothes, I have this kind of cultural fix as a resident alien. But over there also, even when dressed in a very horrible way, an Indian way . . . you know. And that's very nice. I don't mind that. I don't mind not being at home in either of the places. I was asked at one point, by a very close woman friend of mine who lives in Australia (but has a small son and she was thinking of perhaps going back to India to settle in terms of her son's upbringing)—she said, "Well, you know, Gayatri, you've lived abroad for so long, especially as a woman, what do you think? What is better?" And I'd never really thought about it in those terms before. And asked by someone to whom I was close, and was really asking it, not in terms of cultural stereotyping, I gave it some thought and then I said to her, "You know,

Kaveri, both are bad, but in different ways." And then, you know, I'm kind of a demagogic person so I like to make little aphorisms, so I made up this one. I said, "Well, you know, I have a mother and that's Calcutta, and I have a very nurturing stepmother and that's the United States. Both are ugly. On the other hand, if your mother is ugly, and your stepmother is almost, as I said, a nurturing stepmother, you can't just throw her away." So that to an extent, I feel I've earned the right to critique two places.

A   Two mothers?

GCS   Yes. So that's how I feel. I am bicultural, but my biculturality is that I'm not at home in either of the places.

A   . . . It is comfortable. When we lived in what used to be "Rhodesia", I was glad I hadn't been born there; when I got back to England I was glad that I was very much an outsider because I was a filthy colonial, as far as they could tell, and in America the same thing. But I am white. This is not "I'm guilty because I'm white." I'm white because my mother made me like this, but what's so interesting about your position, and about Indian Americans, is that that doesn't count. Our Egyptian friend is much lighter than you, though she has this very Semitic nose.

GCS   But she also has a *much* more convincing British accent than I do.

A   But she feels all sorts of discrimination in this country. Now, she was "used to it" at Cambridge. But she went down to the Caribbean last year and they had to stop off in Puerto Rico for seven hours, and she told me when she got back, "I felt so comfortable there; everybody's the same colour I am." Now I've *never* heard her say anything like that.

GCS   Yes, but that's another thing I felt in India, that I was recognizably—I'm using the word "upper class" because I hate Indians who marginalize themselves.

A   Here?

GCS   Anywhere. They say "middle class". I mean the fact that I didn't have running hot water at home when I grew up, that the food was cooked on a bucket of coals, there was no refrigerator, doesn't mean I wasn't upper class. You understand? So this is another thing from that eccentric business: in India, whatever I do, I'm recognisable, marked socially as, you know, "up there". And also, of course, I felt that there was no way that there could be any kind of racism against me, and I have never taught anywhere in the world where that thing was not there.

A   Anyone you held hands with had the same color hand?

GCS   It's not a question of colour. It's more complicated.

A Isn't it? That's why I found the story about colour in Puerto Rico so remarkable. So tell me.

GCS It's the thing about citizenship that I was talking about. That's why I brought in the class thing first. In India it was unquestioned class privilege, and then, of course, no one was discriminating against me because I did not look like a tribal, or poor. So this, I felt, as I say, was a very good thing. But nonetheless, I also felt that, here, when I encounter something which might look somewhat like racism, it's a useful thing. I don't like it in Britain, you know because of this real strong racism.

A Getting even worse, I think?

GCS It's getting worse. I'm definable. Here it's an indefinable thing, and one thing that one can do here (because of the thing about Indians being different here) is that no one can really not be exercised on one's own behalf. One can really think about other people. And that, too, is an historical thing. Whereas in India because I'm so recognisably upper class, there's not this not being exercised on one's own behalf.

I've never been afraid of intervening, speaking out, even when I came here in '61 as a member of a foreign students group. I was interviewed for *Newsweek*. I am on the cover of *Newsweek*, April, 1963. Here I was, hardly making two ends meet. I'd no money. First year I wasn't given a fellowship, because my first language wasn't English.

A Say that again.

GCS Yes. The first year I went to Cornell. You know first in First Class from the University of Calcutta.

A And you didn't get a fellowship because your first language wasn't English? Although you spoke better English than any American university student.

GCS Well, I spoke English pretty much as I do now. And one should recognise the University of Calcutta, after all, is what was then the cultural centre of the British Empire as it were, outside of the white dominions. It was a bit ridiculous. But nonetheless I borrowed money, on what used to be called a "life mortgage", and came. But as I was being interviewed by these blokes, I had absolutely no compunction in producing this deathless line. I only know it because I got hate mail you wouldn't believe. I said—and I was being honest because I felt that I should say what I thought—"I don't understand why Americans who don't know you smile at you on the street. I've been traumatized." Can you imagine? Really. This was a very genuine kind of a thing. I now know that it was an astute thing to say. I was a luscious nineteen-year-old, and they smiled at me because, to an extent, they didn't really think. It's like women in *National Geographic* where they are allowed to have bare breasts. I was not someone with whom they had the same rules, the same sexual code of behaviour. So it was okay. But you know, that comes from two things. One is the fact that I was a "communist" so early, right? So I kind of felt politics in other people. But also a communist out of moral outrage. But it also comes from a very bad thing, which is my caste-fix. Brahmin women have always been outspoken.

A In India?

GCS In India. Where do you have Brahmin women? I mean they cease to be that adjective. It no longer applies as an explanatory model; it just becomes a descriptive term once you go outside India. My recent marriage is with a Brahmin man, and in fact I found out from the service— since we decided to have a bogus Hindu marriage since I wasn't carrying my divorce papers—that as far as my culture-fix is concerned it was the first time that I was married because I was at last given in exchange. Yes. There is possibility of exchange only when there can be a qualitative equalization.

A Would that be the same if the other men you had married were lower-caste Indian men?

GCS No.

A It's completely outside the system. It doesn't count?

GCS It doesn't count. It's whoring or it's nothing. My younger sister is married to an extraordinarily successful, very intelligent, kind, good man who happens to be of the second caste. It's not a marriage, you know, according to very orthodox standards.

A And are there very orthodox standards?

GCS Of course there are. If there are standards, they're orthodox. That's the whole thing about the institution of marriage. You see, it's like "Home-Owning". You know when you ask me about it, I'm not interested in denigrating a Third World country in terms of the enlightened West. Which is why when you asked me about my hair I immediately talked about leg-hair. It can be a sign of 1960s feminism. It can also be other things. In the same way, when one owns "a home", as the word goes.

A They say "home" in this country; it's only in America.

GCS I know. And why is the housing index something that's always cited in the business pages? Because it's the largest amount of capital that an individual releases into the circuit of capital. So you are rewarded fiscally and so on. So that all that stuff about how wonderful it is to really have a home with someone you truly love, and how those in radical partnership arrangements, lesbian marriages, gay marriages, etc., or

heterosexual non-institutionalized marriages, declare solidarity by buying "a home". In fact the standards are the old circuit of industrial
capitalism's standards. So if there are standards, they're old, they're
orthodox standards. It's the same.

You know, I said a bit ago, that it really depends on what one does
with being white which is much more interesting, because being white
you have to do more if you really want to be politically correct. Whereas
I can have an alibi, although, born a Brahmin, upper-class, senior academic in the United States, highly commodified distinguished professor,
what do you want?

A "Highly commodified distinguished professor". That's good.

GCS Right. Not *as* commodified, let's say, as Hillis Miller or Stanley
Fish, or Frederic Jameson, all my friends, but nonetheless, commodified.
I still have an alibi. My skin. And you don't.

A I'm a lesbian, though. Can't I use that? No. I can't. It doesn't
"show".

GCS Right. You have to wear a T-shirt. I don't have to wear anything.
So it's the same argument that I make about women. There's no reason
why one should, in terms of all the stratification, say that being a man
is bad, just as being a white is bad.

A Well, and one can't help it, ultimately.

GCS And it depends on what you *do*, or, also, where you're placed.
That's the kind of thing that I have discovered more and more. But I was
going to say something much more interesting, really infinitely more
interesting than this. It was something about feminism and the constituency of feminism.

Well, you were going to ask me about native language. Okay, I'll tell
you something about native language. I, although I say so myself, am
pretty good at my native language. It's not just that I speak it; I give
public lectures, and I write in it, and so on.

A And they ask you how the hell you learned it so well.

GCS No, they don't. Yes, some people ask me, but my cronies know.
But, and I think this is very, very important, I found out this time, that
there is one thing I couldn't do in my native language, which was have
a serious fight involving psycho-sexual, social issues. A serious fight.
That's the one thing where I have been *absolutely* affected by the traffic
with Western man. I can sort of do it now, but it's not on the same terms,
the exchange.

A Well, you left when you were nineteen.

GCS Yes. I was sexually active, but never had those serious kinds

. . .

A   That's very much one of those stages of growing up.

GCS   Yes. And I can do it now, but when I fight in my native language now, have a serious fight in my native language, it's a different person. I mean, it's what I was talking about in terms of using Foucault's second volume of *The History of Sexuality*. I realised through this relationship to my language that indeed it counts in terms of what sexuality as a word, as a referent—and Foucault is very determined that he's not talking about signifiers—sexuality as a referent is fixed elsewhere in the language. Now that, I would *never* have known. It just blew me away, but it's absolutely true.

On the other hand, if I had been one of those upper-class Indians— thousands of them around, who really do not speak their native language, except to chit-chat, or speak to their servants; they speak to each other in English—I would never have known.

A   When you were a child, was there a sort of slippage into English?

GCS   No. I went even to a Bengali medium school, and instruction was given in Bengali until high school. No, there was no ease with English anywhere. I mean there was English in one class, in school, but I can't imagine speaking in English to any of my family, except of course, my American niece & nephew, with whom I *also* speak in Bengali. In fact, I find it extremely difficult to speak to another Bengali in English.

A   What about to someone who's not a Bengali? What about someone from Bihar or Punjab?

GCS   Well, that's another thing that I felt in India. You see, I speak Hindi quite badly. I speak it, but I speak it *quite* badly and that's the national language, and I don't know any of the South Indian languages. So that I am much more comfortable, from the point of view of language, let's say, in France, than I am in Delhi. India is not a place. It's really a sort of political construct.

A   Well, it's like Africa. Sub-Saharan Africa?

GCS   Sure. But on the other hand, talking to me, you wouldn't really think that I'm kind of totally marked by the same cultural construct as someone from sub-Saharan Africa, would you?

A   No, no. I meant . . .

GCS   But I am. I am, is what I'm saying.

A   Well, probably that was the wrong thing to say. Because in terms of language, in Africa actually there are speakers of French, and Portuguese . . .

GCS   Well, in terms of who owned what parts. The British owned almost everything except small corners of India. But that's not the problem. Not everyone, in spite of what the guide books say, speaks English. And anyway the interesting stuff is not in English. I'll tell you a very simple story. Running. In Delhi, when I run (and I never saw a woman my age running. Much younger and maybe I saw *two*.)

A   Do men run?

GCS   Yes, but men also run like platypi. Platypuses. Platypoi? But, in Delhi, where I couldn't speak too well—and everyone would *look*; that was okay—but older men, you know, upper-class people, would walk up very close to me and they would spit. And the only thing that I devised, was that I would look into their eyes and I would spit. This used to really blow them away. But on the other hand in Calcutta, people wouldn't spit, they would say things, and I would turn to them and I would say *horrible* things in extremely elegant obscene Bengali . . . like, "You weren't dropped from your mother's womb," and so on. It doesn't sound so good when you say it in Bengali.

A   And you can say those things in Bengali?

GCS   Of course I can. I can say anything.

A   It's just the having a fight that you can't . . .

GCS   Yes. I know street language very well. I grew up there. And, you know, people would say things like, "Male or female?" Because I was that tall.

A   What did you wear, when you ran?

GCS   Shorts. And I'd say, "Well, you know, you look at the chest development, but you're too short." I could do all of this stuff in Bengali, but in Delhi, all I could do was spit. That's the kind of difference that I'm talking about. You really feel that you're in a foreign country.

I mean, that's *all* I could do in Delhi. I did not have the sharp edge of a language with which I could decimate them and tell them to blast off.

A   It had just to be physical?

GCS   It had to be physical. On buses, for example, women my age, would say—not knowing that I was a Bengali, because I was as I was. You know, it's very hard to tell, if I were wearing Delhi clothes, right?— "Very hard to tell if this is male or female."

A   What are Delhi clothes?

GCS   You know, the tight Indian trousers and top. And then in Calcutta I would say to them *very* loudly, "It's not right; it's not polite to discuss people in public in this way." And then, one or two times the women would say, "Sorry. We didn't realise you were Bengali". I'd say, "So, it's only when you're found out that you're polite, is it? What did your parents teach you?" But I can't do that in Hindi.

A   And that problem never arises in either English- or French-speaking countries?

GCS   Yes it does. I am quite often called "Sir" here, and I'm called "m'sieur" in French.

A   But the language. You can cut people down in French and in English—can you?—as happily as you can in Bengali?

GCS   Well, in Bengali, I'm happier, because that's the one sense of being at home. I really feel nobody can do anything to me, whereas here, I'm careful.

A   Are you?

GCS   Of course I am.

A   Do you mean it?

GCS   Yes I am; of course I am. Not because I want to be, but it's sort of that one even notices; those friends who are not racist, one in fact *notices* that they're not racist. You know?

A   That's another of those things I don't know, because racism in this country comes from white people.

GCS   It's a very complicated thing. And in fact those friends who *think* they're not racist are not always racists. So it's a very complicated thing and it's not that you *want* to be careful, but you are careful.

The other day I did something. (You see, I use positions of power. I told the story about Saudi Arabia, when I was in the men's university, where no woman had ever given a faculty development thing, but my enlightened Saudi male host had dragged me in *sub rosa*. At the women's centre there were three hundred people, and no air-conditioning. And at the men's centre—fifteen men, huge ampitheatre, air-conditioning, television cameras, but they were reading newspapers. I thought, "What the hell should I do?" They obviously had been dragged there. And I asked myself, "What position of power do they acknowledge?" And I thought, "mother". And so I started talking to them. "There are *so* few here! Perhaps we could begin by talking about where we went to school, and what we do." And you know, once I started talking that way, they didn't know what to think.

So, it is true, I feel, that I have to use something like this. Mothership, or an accent.)

The other day I was trying to back out of a position between two cars on my street. (I own a home; I'm a "home-owner".) I couldn't back out because the two cars were very close together, and as I was doing it—it was on a slope, and I have a gear-shift car—I was touching the car behind me. The white guy from the adjoining house started screaming at me. I was so pissed off, and I think it was "property". I felt I own a house on this street; that is a position of power. And then the mother thing came in. I waved my insurance card, and I said, "Look. You want my insurance number? Come and get it. If not, move your bloody car so I can get out." Because there was room behind him. So he comes down sort of muttering, and it was a hot day and my window rolled down, and I said to him, in this very motherly tone and a very English accent, "*Stop muttering.*" And he was so amazed, that someone dressed like me had said to him, also a homeowner, "Stop muttering"—and in my totally battered car—he stopped muttering. And he backed up, and I passed out. And I felt that it was a victory, because it's very hard for me to do this kind of thing here.

A   I'm afraid that in America, English accents—

GCS   Ah, white. I've now remembered what the point was. It really does depend not so much on whiteness but on what kind of passport you hold. [?] I'll tell you two things. My mother has a U.S. passport. Because my brother does. She's seventy-four. She's a heroic woman, but in her appearance, she's short; she certainly doesn't look like anything but a seventy-four-year-old Bengali widow. I took her to France for a birthday present. I was a guest of the government—College Internationale—they paid my fare. And there was my mother; she spoke no French. I spoke French; I went under scrutiny. And my mother, waving her American passport, walked through. To an extent, it really is *not* ultimately skin colour. You should speak to people from Central America, Latin America, with whom Hispanics in this country want completely to identify. They speak bitterly about the fact that the don't recognise them, that it does make a difference; it's not just ethnic.

A   But doesn't that pertain only when one is at a border? I don't carry my passport. Do you carry your passport?

GCS   No. I carry—

A   Your little card—

GCS   Yes. But that is such an important thing, freedom to move. There are in the world also passports which do not allow you to move. Think of South Africa.

A   Think of this country when Americans weren't allowed to go to Cuba, China, several other places.

GCS   Yes, but by choice. It wasn't that those places stopped them.

A   No, but America wouldn't let them go.

GCS   But that's a very different thing. A very different thing.

What has happened to me now is that I am much more interested in looking at Indians as in the subject position. Rather than as an object of investigation. My husband's an historian of India, and he feels that to teach Indian history elsewhere is like what I was calling "information retrieval" teaching, and what he calls being a technician. And although he says, "I have no stake, no material stakes in this country" (and he's even less patriotic than I am), he says, "At least when I teach the subject here, I feel that I am teaching, rather than giving information." I feel the same way about teaching in the United States, that I am *not* giving information. Because through my work in lit. crit., Marxism, feminism, what it has come to now is a critique of imperialist cultural politics. Right? You can *only* teach it in the bosom of the superpower. Elsewhere, it's about "other people". As to what effect it has, is not the point. Here you teach it as a subject; elsewhere, you teach it as information retrieval. I do feel that I do that with the U.S. as in the position of the subject. Therefore, I want to continue to teach in the United States.

But, on the other hand, I think about the critique of imperialism, which never was an apology for India, but had almost began to become that. Now, in India, people who can think of the three-worlds explanation are totally pissed off by not being recognised as the centre of the non-aligned nations, rather than a "Third-World" country.

When I think about Indians, now—this is again, finally, the biculturalism that happened God knows how, which really now comes to inhabit my academic, intellectual work—there is a very productive split. The fact that what I teach in terms of the critique of imperialism and the cultural politics of that, that the United States is in the subject position, is now, I think, very productively in crisis with the fact that I also think of Indians in the subject position in terms of their collaboration. I mean, let's take a hypothetical case. An Indian female research assistant, who is incompetent and irresponsible—

A   In America—

GCS   In America—has been wished on me because of the great white fathers' thinking that I should be den mother of the subcontinental ghetto, right? But, clearly, and having been an Indian student myself, for reasons that are not India's fault, we are not well trained in first-class computerized libraries. So let's say that this hypothetical, female, somewhat self-aggrandising, politically full-of-herself research assistant does not know how to be a research assistant in the United States. And let's say that I understand this. I do not hold it against her; I push her towards an introduction to bibliography, independent study, etc., because it's not her fault. But then it emerges that this person is also highly irresponsible. Then suppose this person, an Indian woman, writes a *long* letter saying that I am doing a power play because she's Indian and I cannot relate to Indian women. I will judge her as a subject.

In the same way that there are—again a hypothetical case—white Marxists in this country who do not get tenure. But let us assume that this person did not get tenure because he was always looking for fellowships and so on at very privileged universities, so that he was never *in* his home university. He never taught there. So he didn't get tenure. And he said, very much in public, that he didn't get tenure because he was a Marxist. It's kind of comparable. Now, it is true that Marxists do not get tenure because they are Marxists. That has nothing to do with this person. And it is absolutely conceivable that it is true that I might have difficulty relating to an Indian woman, in my workplace, because I've always taught in the United States, mostly white students, or at least U.S. students. Both of these things might be true. Nonetheless, the subject positions from which these explanations are coming are not "I am incompetemt," but "I'm an Indian"; and not "I'm out for the main chance", but "I'm a Marxist." In both cases one should be able to judge by taking these people as subjects and I think *now* I am in that position.

A   Well, thank goodness you didn't wait until you were sixty-five and feeling sort of cranky, creaky, before you went back to India.

GCS   No, then no one would have spat at me.

A   If you'd run around in shorts at the age of sixty-five, God knows, they'd probably have got their machetes out. You obviously did it at the right time.

GCS   Yes, I'm very pleased.

A   If you'd been in your say, middle thirties.

GCS   It's always the right time.

A   I don't know. I've had rather radical changes in my life but they've been times at which I've switched continents, and I can never tell whether it's my age or moving from continent to continent.

GCS   Tres [at the time of the interview a graduate student in the University of Texas, Austin], who can get into this interview by name, knows how the desire to teach in India came about. It was when my second long-term sexual companion left me, and in a *complete* sexist, ethnicist, ideological funk, I said to myself, "I must go home." That was truly, if you don't mind my saying so, a piece of shit. But it was out of that, which was in 1981, because these things move slowly (I do not have an Indian degree beyond the B.A.), that finally the History Centre invited me. (I don't have any sort of history degree anywhere.) It took six years, and I'm very pleased it did because in those six years I was completely over that funk. I mean, I certainly did not go back thinking I was going *home*. I was going to teach. And for the first time I had a bank account in India. I said to my mother, "Can you imagine, Ma? For the first time". I did coaching in English in 1959 and '60 and '61; that's not the same thing.

A   It's not real.

GCS   It's not real. You get it in cash. And I told my mother that. "I can't believe that I actually have a bank account. I'm paid by cheque. Extraordinary." But if I had gone ahead to run out of this—

A   You'd just have been a mess, and formed, one assumes, all sorts of wrong impressions.

GCS   Yes, and I would have gone on with that white—one can't say "black" in this country—white/Indian, totally nonsensical divide. You know, white male companion; going home to India. If there's one thing I totally distrust, in fact, more than distrust, despise and have contempt for, it is people looking for roots. Because anyone who can conceive of looking for roots, should, already, you know, be growing rutabagas.

A   Well, as far as American are concerned, I assume though I don't *know*, it became "an Idea," and it was probably rather a misplaced idea: But looking for roots, no; one carries one's roots.

GCS   And everyone has roots. Why look for them?

A   Yes. We carry them around; they're right here.
[Pause]

GCS   This is very important. This is the citizenship business. People say constantly, it's hard to understand me, right? Now here, I really feel that, given the most opulent university system in the world, where clearly the humanities have as an ideology know-nothingism, so that they cannot be critical in this society, their definition of elitism is where their understanding stops. Where your comprehension stops, elitism begins. This is it. So here—don't forget, I became an assistant professor in 1965; I've taught here for a *very* long time and always at non-prestigious schools—I have always said to people here, "Look, you're an academic. Do your homework. If I weren't supposed to teach you something, why are you in class?" In India, on the other hand, since I'd been asked to teach what I'd been asked to teach, I felt, since it was a different institution, access to education was different, I was obliged to *make* myself understood. Because these things change; these things are not transcendental. I wasn't justifying the fact that I spoke one way. These things change in different contexts. And so I worked harder on my courses there than I have ever done in my entire life. My entire teaching has changed as a result of teaching in a place where I was a citizen and all that stuff, where I did not to an extent feel that the institution was not something that I could really, seriously intervene in. That has changed.

A   And so this semester now at Pittsburgh is really different?

GCS   Definitely. And with the teaching I'm doing, I feel that I'm really teaching about as well as I can. Mind you it's a seminar only on Marx.

A   And only a seminar means how many people?

GCS   Twenty. I really felt in India that it was my obligation to make myself [understood]. And people in fact comment on the fact that I seem much more lucid.

A   You said in your talk this afternoon that you had been very "personal". Has that changed? I mean has the personal thing changed?

GCS   Well, I have always felt that one should speak personally. Yes, that one should think of oneself as a public individual, so that it's not like every bit of your confessional history, but it's trying to think of the representative space which you occupy. But now I feel that I can talk about that representative space with more authority because I have been around in a place where people can really check me out rather than think of me as a piece of exotica. It's true.

A   Good.

GCS   It's very nice to be able to say my generation's approaching fifty now.

Anyway, that's it, Angela. It's unresolved. . . .

8

Practical Politics of
The Open End

This interview was recorded in Pittsburgh, Pennsylvania, where Gayatri Spivak is an Andrew Mellon Professor of English, on October 31/November 1, 1987. First published in Canadian Journal of Political and Social Theory/Revue canadienne de théorie politique et sociale, Vol. 12, No. 1–2, 1988.

HARASYM   In a number of your essays ("Scattered Speculations on the Question of Value," for example[5]) you discuss the history of the epistemic violence of imperialism as crisis management. I would like to begin with two questions: To what extent does the question of value when it is determined by the "idealist" predication of the subject as consciousness and/or by the "materialist" predication of the subject as labor power manage the crisis of imperialism? Could you outline what some of the theoretico-political or politico-theoretical implications/problems are that arise when the question of value is determined by a "materialist" subject predication such as Marx's?

SPIVAK   What we have to keep in mind when we are thinking of the so-called "idealist" and the so called "materialist" predication is that these two adjectives can never be entertained as final. But, any way, if we decide we are going to make a distinction between them, we have to remember that "value," the word "value," the concept or the metaphor "value," means two different things in the two different contexts. Very loosely speaking, in the context where the human being is defined with consciousness as its specifically defining characteristic or, to put it on another register, where the subject is predicated as consciousness, if we call it the idealist predication, in that context, the word "value" means, in shorthand, the old fashioned three values: "Truth," "Beauty," "Goodness"—Weber's or Habermas's three value spheres, cognitive, aesthetic, ethical. So that basically what we see is that the part of the world which implicitly claims that the history of human consciousness has found its best fulfillment in it is, also, the *site* which is the home of the axiological, the home of the values. And the rest of the world is measured against that. So that, in fact, to qualify for the subjectship of ethics, that can choose between right and wrong imagining that it is *the* human subject, one must be located in that part of the world where the history of human consciousness has found its fulfillment. So that even access to critique of the position is available, for example, through a position like *mine*, a position which has gone through the itinerary. The crisis of the other part of the world wanting perhaps to claim, or the possibility of their wanting to claim, that they have indigenous homes for an axiological program, can be managed by this particular presupposition. So that one says, for example, that access to critique of this kind is, again, through the cultural itinerary of imperialism and so on. That's crisis management from the so-called "idealist" predication: consciousness as the defining predicate of the human being.

On the other hand, if you take the so called "materialist" predication of the subject as work, work which subsumes consciousness within it as, also, *a* kind of work, value is that mediating, and to quote Marx, the "slight and contentless" [*Capital*, Vol. 1] "Inhaltlos" thing: the mediating and "contentless" differential which can never appear on its own, but it is always necessary in order to move from labor to commodity, in order to move from labor to the possibility of its products being exchanged. Now if this is ignored, and it has been ignored, dismissed, for example, by economists who have wanted to claim Marxism back into the discipline of economics—I'm speaking now of, let's say, the Sraffians. If one attends to this instead of ignoring it as either "metaphysical" or too "starry-eyed political" or not theoretically astute enough, if one attends to this "slight and contentless thing" that is the mediating possibility between labor and commodity and the possibility of exchange—and I'm not going to spell out the whole argument for you because this *is* Marx's basic argument—if it is attended to, then there is a possibility of suggesting to the worker that the worker produces capital, that the *worker* produces capital because the worker, the container of labor power, is the source of value. By the same token it is possible to suggest to the so-called "Third World" that it *produces* the wealth and the possibility of the cultural self-representation of the "First World."

This afternoon at a women's graduate student's conference where I was running the workshop on international students, there was present a small group of young white American women who clearly with a lot of benevolence, but completely unexamined benevolence, were suggesting that there was perhaps something wrong in our not acknowledging that we were getting all of these benefits of the U.S. education system, that we were only talking about our problems within the institution. I argued then, following this argument, although I tried to keep it as unpolitically vocabularized as possible, I argued then that if one looked at the documents of the International Monetary Fund and the World Bank, if one actually looked at the way in which budgets were established, etc., one would know that to an extent the position from where the U.S. educational system, the university system is able to make itself so technically and qualitatively well endowed, a lot of it is produced by the "Third World", and if you want to work it out, you have to work it out from the argument of value: that "slight and contentless" mediating differential between labor power and commodity. Now, the way in which it is produced, on the other hand, is not visible because most people do not read those kinds of economic documents. What they read is ideological stuff in journals and newspapers written by people who are not aware of this fully. On the other hand, the fact that all of these foreign students are at universities is eminently visible, and the fact that they will go back and themselves perhaps work to keep this crisis management intact is an added bonus. But, it is only through the argument that there is this contentless, mediating differential which allows labor power to valorize value that is, the possibility of exchange and surplus, that we can grasp that the manipulation of Third World labor sustaining the continued resources of the U.S. academy which produces the ideological supports for that very manipulation.

If one attends to this—and I'm really sorry if in order to make this "absolutely" transparently clear I would really have to say, "Just read Marx's texts carefully." Those thousands and thousands of pages, in fact, explain only this over and over again to the implied reader: who is, of course, the worker within capital logic. Just know that *you* produce capital, and you can only know this if you forget about your concrete experience simply as what gives you the picture of the world. Think it through and you will see that you are producing capital, and no one is giving you anything like money or wages in exchange for something. In fact, what you are getting is produced by you and it's being shuffled back to you so more of it can be produced to keep the capitalist alive. O.K. That's what the so-called materialist predication of the subject as labor power can do in terms of our understanding crisis management. It really changes the subject position, altogether, whereas, the "idealist" predication manages the crisis by saying that the history of consciousness found its fulfillment in this part of the globe. If you don't attend to it, attend to this value question, then, of course, you work back . . . you fall back into the notion that the "First World" countries are helping the "Third World" countries to develop, and, of course, you don't really have to be this theoretical to know that if you simply read the appropriate documents you will see that each aid package comes with certain kinds of requirements for buying certain kinds of goods, percentage of the nationality of workers on the different levels that can be employed this way or that, etc. It's too obvious even to enumerate. But, in fact, when you don't read that, and you believe that you are helping the other side of the world develop itself, the philosophical argument that can make you understand that it is exactly the other way around, is the notion of the concept-metaphor of value and this can be explained in class to students. I would say that that's how the two predictions relate to the crisis management of imperialism.

You ask me what might be some of the problems. I think part of the problem might be to turn the theory of value into an analogy for consciousness which is done by many theoretical people, or, on the other side, if you decide to identify value with price rather quickly. That can make a real problem and that can be done if you don't read this carefully enough. The final problem that can arise is to feel that only value-producing work, work that produces commodities that can be exchanged, or, which is even worse, work that produces value that can valorize itself—which is capitalism—is real work. If you feel that only value producing work is real work that's a problem, or on the other side, if you feel that only use-values, that goods that are produced for consumption by the producer, that only that is good, that's a problem.

HARASYM   Over the past few months, there have appeared in Canadian newspapers a number of articles about the "forgiveness" of debt to "Third World" countries. Is this so called "benevolent" gesture of "forgiveness" the management of a crisis?

SPIVAK   Well, you see that the way in which the answer to this question has to be considered is by looking at, as I have said—there is an ideological relation between that a set of newspapers, what a set of government documents that are released for publication and what you find in the actual document of the World Bank and the I.M.F. The forgetting, the forgiving of public debt—what one has to look at are what are the conditions that ride on these particular things that are being described as being forgiven. In order to see how crisis is managed, you would have to see—this is absolutely incumbent upon someone who wants to do this kind of theorizing (as in any case, to be a theorist of something, you have to look at the documentation in detail)—that's what has to be looked at, at the individual cases as they are presented in hard terms rather than as what the public policy statements are. I follow this more in the case of India than in the case of other countries, and I'm always struck by analyses of what is said: how it's represented to the general Indian public, how it is represented to the First World countries, and what, in fact, it looks like if you look at the details of each of those gestures.

HARASYM   To many contemporary Marxist (deconstructive and/or feminist) thinkers Marx's mode of production narrative is problematic.

Although Marx deals in a very schematic way with the problem of colonization, it would appear that Marx's mode of production narrative is,
perhaps, complicit with the imperialist project. How do you approach
this narrative in your work?

SPIVAK   If we want the proper development toward international socialism to take place, we must put every country through the regular
stages of one mode of production following the other, and where we
have an example of such a thing is in Western Europe. This is basically
the understanding of Marx's argument upon which is predicted the
notion that it is complicit with imperialism. Capitalism is a way to . . .
monopoly capitalist imperialism as a way to bring social change into
the countries so that they could move toward socialism. Now I would
certainly not disagree that there is a certain plausibility of this. If one
looks not only at the Lenin-Luxenburg debates or the various kinds of
writing on imperialism that have been produced by first and second
generations of Marxism involved in politics. Although I would not say
that there is such a possibility, I would also say that if one looked at the
writings then of people a generation later—Victor Kiernan or Harry
Magdoff—one begins to realize that that is only one way of dealing with
Marxism and the question of imperialism. Then, if one goes even further
and back to Marx, then one can see in order to produce a reading which
is politically more useful, rather than a reading would simply throw
away an extremely powerful analysis because it can be given a certain
kind of reading, one would see that in the postface to *Capital* I, for
example, what Marx says is that Germany could not develop political
economy because in Germany capitalism is not developed in the way it
developed in England. So then, Marx says, it is not possible for Germany
to develop political economy, the professors of political economy in
Germany are creating nonsense out of the paratheoretical petit bourgeois
consciousness, but there *is* a possibility in Germany for a critique of
political economy. Because the discipline could not develop in Germany
critique cannot be located in the bosom of the theorists, it will come
from the disenfranchised. The relationship between Marxism and the
developing countries might usefully be drawn on this model. There has
also been a certain "historical" tendency toward ignoring the problem of
women within revolutionary protocol that has more to do with what I
said in answer to the first question. That there is a tendency to assume
that the "materialist" predication of the subject means that only value-
producing work, or only that work which produces self-valorizating
value, is real work. It is repeatedly said by Marx, that to make that
identification is estrangement. In fact, whenever Marx tries—certainly
in the early Marx, but it is also in the later Marx—whenever Marx tries
to find an example of how to understand this estrangement outside of

capital logic, he thinks about the relation between men and women. You can say that Marx is a heterosexist, but that you can say about many feminists, too, who are not necessarily prejudiced against male or female homosexuality but who occupy a heterosexist position. That's a different issue. To say that Marx in fact said that value-producing work was the only real work, or that work that produces self-valorizing value was the only real work, and, therefore, ignored the relationship between men and women—it is almost like saying, on an analogy, psychoanalysis is no good for literary criticism. When in fact, Freud and Lacan and certain other analysts have looked at literary texts as something that could be an explanatory model for psychoanalysis. I would say that that's at the bottom of the feminist objection, which certainly related to the fact that within revolutionary traditions also there has been room for this misunderstanding. I think, then, what one has to cope with then is the sexism of radicals as well as reactionary males, rather than something *specifically* wrong with Marxism or with the modes of production narrative. And I think if you take the modes of production narrative as a norm, to the extent Jameson does, Jameson—whose work I admire greatly in many ways and whose politics I support greatly in many ways; what happens— and I'm not the only one to say this . . . Apparently (I haven't as yet looked at it. I was in India when it came out) there was a whole issue of *Social Text*[6] which shows a critical position towards his judgement of Third World literature as allegories of nationalism. Now that comes from taking the modes of production narrative as normative because nationalism, itself, which is very much within a certain history of European—norm is seen as an unquestioned good that these "Third World" countries should now be aspiring to. That's a problem.

Now another thing that one could find in Marx, for example is a morphology which talks about self-valorizing value as a kind of *thing* whose form of appearance [*Erscheinungs form*] you see in the history of the development of the modes of production of value. You see how value valorizes itself. What happens, O.K., that's morphological semi-narrative. To back this up, you have various 18th-century styles where everything fits—you've seen this in Rousseau, you've seen this in Condillac, you've seen this in all the great 18th-century Enlightenment proto-anthropological thinkers who make a certain kind of very broad stroke, universal narrative fit with a morphological argument. But, that's not all there is to Marx. When Marx goes toward discussing actual "historical" events like his discussion of 1848, like his journalistic stuff, you see that the moment he talks about these kinds of narratives, the relationship between the normative morphology and the unfolding narratives becomes much more ambivalent. So that one can't just take Marx in terms of the first two things.

So you ask me what I do with the modes of production narratives? Well, I, since my general tendency—this is an idea I have published elsewhere and it would take too long really to hold forth on it at the moment[7]—since I really believe that given our historical position that we have to learn to negotiate with structures of violence, rather than taking the impossible elitist position of turning our backs on everything. In order to be able to talk to you, in order to be able to teach within the bosom of the superpower, in order to be, in whatever way, as a citizen of India, some kind of corrective voice towards nativist cultural history there, I have to learn myself and teach my students to negotiate with colonialism itself. I say to upwardly class-mobile feminists, generally the leaders, to learn to negotiate with phallocentricism because they do it anyway. In the same way, I look at this narrative of the modes of production and I negotiate with it, rather than simply take it as normative, or say that if I were to take it as normative my hands would not be clean. As if one could *not* take it as normative living as one does. One's own social relations prove over and over again that whatever one says, however, one makes *visible* the normativity of that narrative. Therefore, one must learn to negotiate.

HARASYM   Since the 1960s one of the questions addressed by French post-structuralist thinkers is how to combine the contributions of post-structuralist thought with a Marxist/feminist program. To what extent is this gesture in its turn the management of a crisis? Where would you situate your work on the critique of imperialism and on the heterogeneous production of the gendered subaltern subject in relation to this gesture?

SPIVAK   Well, you see everything is crisis management in a certain sense. One could make it an extremely broad category. The management of crisis is not necessarily a bad thing. I think it includes, as Derrida would say, the "ethical" as well as the "non-ethical." It seems to me that the most important contribution of post-structuralist thought towards the projects of Marxism as they understood it, has been to point out the presence of metaphysical categories in Marx. It has taught me—and you know how much I have learned from that essay by Derrida, "The Ear of the Other."[8] Well before I had read this essay, in my early two essays on Marx after Derrida, I was looking for critical moments in Marx that would open up his texts to something other than simply a program set down by these metaphysical presuppositions. I think that's one of the strong contributions of post-structuralism, and, later, when you ask me that question about "practice," I will come back to this. I think, also, the insistence that a subject does not always act in his own interest, most of the post-structuralists have talked about this, that the nature of the subject, thanks to psychoanalysis, is marked by a bar or by an oblique itinerary so that one cannot, in fact, identify the product of epistemologi-cal cleansing and the constituency of social justice. But, as De Man says in that wonderful sentence, "You cannot blame anatomy for not curing mortality." If we paid attention to that we can't of course get our elegant solutions. In fact, the solutions become nonsensical after awhile, after you have chosen them they fall apart. The contribution of post-structural-ism to feminism has been simply the critique of phallocentricism itself. But, then, the historical state of being woman is something that post-structuralism has tried to appropriate a little, in order to articulate for itself a space that is not phallocentric. I think that Derrida's position in the essay called "Geschlect—différence sexuelle, différence ontologique"[9] is somewhat marked—although I do not want to launch into an analysis of this text, but it is somewhat marked by that gesture. I've talked about this at a greater length in essay that is about to appear in a collection edited by Teresa Brennan.[10] That essay is on the relationship between deconstruction and feminism. I would say, yet, that the use of the (histor-ical) figure of the woman is one way to manage the crisis of phallocentri-cism, and even, indirectly of the crisis of the party line communism and socialism in France, if you like. Perry Anderson in *In the Tracks of Historical Materialism*[11] has suggested that because in Marx's thinking itself, the relationship between subject and structure was not clearly thought through, in that fissure post-structuralist notions of subject and practice took root. I don't know what to make of this, but it seems to me that that is also an account of that broad concept-metaphor: crisis management. And here the figure of the woman has been manifestly useful.

I've already articulated how it helps me with Marx. In the context of de-colonization the only things you have to work with, are the great narratives of nationalism, internationalism, secularism, and culturalism. These were *alibis* for decolonization used by that class in the colonies which was, itself, enabled to change the indigenous power structure in terms of what the colonists imposed. They themselves, as not always unwilling objects of a certain kind of epistemic violence, negotiated with these structures of violence in order to emerge as the so-called colonial subject. If in that context and in de-colonized space, one looks at the genuinely disenfranchised who never had access to these grand narra-tives anyway, as a teacher one thinks of a pedagogy on a very generally post-structuralist model: without destroying these narratives, making all of their structures one's own structures, nevertheless, one takes a dis-tance from them and shows what incredible and necessary crimes are attendant upon them: not just aberrations but necessary supplements. One does not, then, produce some kind of legitimizing counter-narrative of nativist continuity. And within this frame, the one most consistently exiled from episteme is the disenfranchised woman, the figure I have called the "gendered subaltern." Her continuing heterogeneity, her continuing subalternization and loneliness, have defined the subaltern subject for me. And I have been helped by the varieties of her representation in the fiction of Mahasweta Devi.[12]

HARASYM   My next question or rather series of questions has to do with institutional responsibility and with the production of knowledge. If, as you write in "Scattered Speculations on the Question of Value," "the complicity between cultural and economic value systems is acted out in almost every decision we make" (166), and if "economic reductionism is, indeed, a very real danger" (166), what place should and do academics occupy within the political economy? What does our institutional responsibility amount to?

SPIVAK   I need an adjective before academics, when you say, "What place should and do academics occupy?" Academics are not homogeneous either. In India, for example, with a nationalized system of education, and access to education much limited by class, the university as a place of classic mobility is both very important and not important. In the United States, where the university system is run more or less like a private enterprise (arguably even in the case of the state universities) you have more than 4,000 tertiary institutions that are extremely heirarchized from junior colleges to senior colleges to your Harvard and Yale. In France, you have a highly centralized nationalist educational system where academic radicalism has taken place almost outside the basic university structure organized by an elitist and homogenizing structure. And so on. It seems to me that there is no such thing as *the* academic, and I think that there is a real danger in identifying one's own position with one of these institutional models, and then thinking of *the* academic. But, given that caution, I would say that in one way or another academics are in the business of ideological production; even academics in the pure science are involved in that process. This possibility leads to the notion of disciplinary as well as institutional situation, and then to the subtler question of precise though often much mediated functions within the institution of a nation state. Thus one cannot canonize one's own discipline and say "I don't have to know, I'm a theoretical physicist" or "I don't have to know I'm a philosopher," etc. Don't canonize the disciplinary divisions of labor. Some of us need to know this. Our institutional responsibility is of course to offer a responsible critique of the structure of production of the knowledge we teach even as we teach it. But, in addition, we must go public as often as we can, especially when we have gained some permanence in the profession.

HARASYM   What political interventional force could or does deconstruction have in the political rewriting of the ethico-political, socio-
historical text and its destination?

SPIVAK   Deconstruction cannot found a political program of any
kind. Deconstruction points out that in constructing any kind of an
argument we must move from implied premises, that must necessarily
obliterate or finesse certain possibilities that question the availability
of these premises in an absolutely justifiable way. Deconstruction
teaches us to look at these limits and questions. It is a corrective and
a critical movement. It seems to me, also, that because of this,
deconstruction suggests that there is no absolute justification of *any*
position. Now, this is not the final say about the position. Deconstruction, also insistently claims that there cannot be a fully practicing
deconstructor. For, the subject is always centered as a subject. You
cannot *decide* to *be* decentered and inaugurate a politically correct
deconstructive politics. What deconstruction looks at is the limits of
this centering, and points at the fact that these boundaries of the
centering of the subject are indeterminate and that the subject (being
always centered) is obliged to describe them as determinate. Politically,
all this does is not allow for fundamentalisms and totalitarianisms
of various kinds, however seemingly benevolent. But it cannot be
foundational. If one wanted to *found* a political project on deconstruction, it would be something like wishy-washy pluralism on the one
hand, or a kind of irresponsible hedonism on the other. That's what
would happen if you changed that morphology into a narrative. Yet
in its suggestion that masterwords like "the worker", or "the woman"
have no literal referents deconstruction is again a political safeguard.

For, when you are *succeeding* in political mobilizations based on the
sanctity of those masterwords, then it begins to seem as if these
narratives, these characteristics, really existed. That's when all kinds
of guilt tripping, card-naming, arrogance, self-aggrandizement and so
on, begin to spell the beginning of an end.

A deconstructive awareness would insistently be aware that the masterwords are catachreses . . . that there are no literal referents, there are
no "true" examples of the "true worker," the "true" examples of the
"true worker," the "true woman," the "true proletarian" who would
actually stand for the ideals in terms of which you've mobilized. The
disenfranchised are quite often extremely irritated with that gesture of
the benevolent towards them which involves a transformation through
definition. They themselves do not like to fit into a category like the
"true worker," "the true woman," etc. I often cite a story by Toni Cade
Bambara, "My Man Bovanne," a story in which she actually deals with
this phenomenon very beautifully. In national liberation movements, for

example, there is a critical moment when a deconstructive vigilance would not allow a movement toward orthodox nationalism.

HARASYM   How is this political interventional force related to what you describe in the final footnote of "Scattered Speculations on the Question of Values" as a practical politics of the open end?

SPIVAK   You will remember that I am talking there of Derrida's essay "Of an Apocalyptic Tone."[13] I made those remarks with reference to a piece that is very abstruse, very beautiful, but extremely difficult, and I'm going to answer you here in as easy a way as I can find. So when you ask me to refer specifically to the last footnote, there will be this gap. I think that a practical politics of the open end can be understood through this analogy. For example, when we actually brush our teeth, or clean ourselves everyday, or take exercise, or whatever, we don't think we are fighting a losing battle against mortality, but, in fact, all of these efforts are doomed to failure because we are going to die. On the other hand, we really think of it much more as upkeep and as maintenance rather than as an irreducibly doomed repeated effort. This kind of activity cannot be replaced by an operation. We can't have a surgical operation which takes care of the daily maintenance of a body doomed to die. That operation would be identical with death. This analogy, like all analogies, is not perfect. It applies to the individual, and if one applied it directly to historical collectivities, one might be obliged to suggest that there are Spenglarian cycles to civilizations. This analogy, itself catechretical, can help us understand the practical politics of the open end. It is not like some kind of massive ideological act (the surgical operation) which brings about a drastic change. Now, in all my thinking about practical politics I have always emphasized that there has to be both these two kinds of things, each—to anticipate something we are going to talk about later— each bringing the other to crisis. Because quite often this tooth-brushing style of daily-maintenance politics seems to require acting out of line. On the other hand, the massive kind of surgery, surgical-operation-type politics which can go according to morphology, seems to deny the everyday maintenance of practical politics. When each brings the other to productive crisis, then it seems to me you have a practical politics of the open end: neither is privileged. In fact, the relationship between feminism and Marxism, the fights that arise, even with people such as Sheila Rowbotham, quite often are based in a misunderstanding of this. So that feminism sees itself as one kind of practical politics wanting, also, to be the other kind. That's just divisiveness, and, just as the disenfranchised "know" that the labels that describe them are catechreti-cal; this kind of practical politics of the open-end, too, is something quite familiar. That's one of the beautiful things about deconstruction: that it really, actually, points at the theoretical implications of the familiar. And so, we in fact know this, but it is always considered an aberration: it is strategically excluded when one is talking theory.

HARASYM   When you were lecturing in Alberta (1986) you gave a very interesting reading of the "living feminine" and the problem of determination in Derrida's text, *The Ear of the Other*. What place does the "living feminine" occupy in this text? Is it structurally similar to the position of the feminine in Derrida's other texts? What is useful in this text to your own work?

SPIVAK   In *The Ear of the Other*, the living feminine seems to me to occupy a place with many other articulations in Derrida's other texts. I think that woman, or the feminine, is a kind of *name* for something in Derrida. It is, as he has insisted elsewhere, neither a figure nor a kind of empirical reality, and the best I have been able to do with my careful reading of his texts is that it is a kind of *name* for something in Derrida. It is, as he has insisted elsewhere, neither a figure nor a kind of empirical reality, and the best I have been able to do with my careful reading of his texts is that it is a kind of name. Just as Foucault in his most interesting texts suggests that power is a name for a certain complex. In the paper that's going to be in the Brennan anthology, I have tried to discuss some of the problems and some of the positive and the useful elements in Derrida's use of the name "woman" for a whole *ensemble* in his morphology: I think the place occupied by the "living feminine" in *The Ear of the Other* is simply the place that stands over against the pact between autobiography and death. The possibility of autobiography is related to death through the fact that autobiography is not life, even biography is not life, and the autobiographer grasps at a name, a name which is bequeathed by the father. What is over against it is the "living feminine, which subtends the nameable, the father's part". O.K. But, if one really wanted to pull out the logic of the concept-metaphor one would see that the "living feminine" once it is named the mother, already has within it a certain kind of repetitive structure. And perhaps, Derrida is looking at *that* when he looks at the contradictions in Nietzsche's texts around the "living feminine." I'm not quite sure of it. I'll have to look at the text again to tell you what I think. It seems to me, also, that in the earlier, much earlier pieces like "Speech and Phenomena,"[14] one of the most interesting things that he shows us is that any conception of a "living present" for the human subject has to assume the subject's death, for this "living present" must have existed before the subject and will exist after the subject. And to an extent, I would feel happier if that kind of thing already encroached into the "living feminine." Otherwise, the "living feminine" becomes a sort of a methodological supposition which is given a name. Now this play between history, the historical place of the name of the mother, as it were, and morphology, the feminine on the other side of difference, etc.—this is what I'm trying to attack in that piece for Teresa Brennan.

What is useful to my own work? I like this text a great deal. What is supremely useful is Derrida's articulation of the new politics of reading: that you do not excuse a text for its historical aberrations, you admit that there is something in the text which can produce these readings. That is extremely useful. But then making the protocols of the text your own, you tease out the critical moments in the text and work at useful readings— readings that are scrupulous re-writings. I have repeated this to students and in talks many times, and I don't want it to become a formula. That's the problem, you know, these wonderful things become formulas, and then people just kind of—it's like a dance step. But, nonetheless, trying to teach Marx this semester, remembering the history of Marxism, re-membering the problems, not trying to excuse Marx or on the other hand, trying to simply turn my back on him, has been a very, very useful, a very productive exercise. I remind myself of this essay as I go on.

HARASYM   In "Imperialism and Sexual Difference"[15] you both borrow and show the limits of borrowing uncritically a strategy of reading articulated by Paul de Man. Please correct me if I am wrong. But, whereas Paul de Man's readings *tend* to stop at various aporias, your readings— here, I am thinking in particular of your work on cultural self-representation—your readings stress the necessity of thinking beyond the aporia as they focus on the situational specific forces of the opposition in order to find a place of practice. What are your thoughts on this reading?

SPIVAK   I think I would partially agree with what you're saying. How-ever, in De Man, the later suggestion: that in order to act you have to literalize the metaphor is important because it takes one beyond the perception of De Man as attempting to reside in an aporia. People like us learned the predicament of discovering an aporia in a text, and then moved in other directions with the aporetic structure. Whereas, since he was articulating it, it took him a long time simply establishing it in text after text, and, in deed, I think it is not to undermine his excellence to say that in the texts of the period of *Allegories of Reading*,[16] one might feel that that's all he is doing. But, I think, again, to read him with a new politics of reading, not to excuse the fact that it can lead in people who are blind followers, into a celebration of what Wlad Godzich,[17] I think incorrectly, although normally I think he is a very astute reader, what he's called "cancelling out" in De Man. I think one can get to a position like that, but, on the other hand, it's also possible to see that in every text there is a signal that aporias are never fully balanced. So that you know that even in the *Allegories of Reading*, the text on Proust, "Reading," when he's discussing metaphor and narrative, you can see that, in fact, in the way he's talking the metaphor is privileged, so that one cannot have a full aporia. De Man always marks the moments of asymmetry in *Allegories of Reading*. But, then, in the later text, "Promises," where he suggests that in order to act you turn the metaphor, you literalize the metaphor, then he's out of simply articulating aporias. This is the work he was on when he died: the work of moving from the description of tropological and performative deconstruction to a definition of the act.

I think you're right when you describe my stuff as you do. Given what I think my usefulness is, I tend to emphasize the asymmetry in terms of the opposition. That's just *my* political style as opposed to theirs. I think without learning from them, this political style would be less, would begin to resemble more and more a kind of old-fashioned understanding of dialectics.

HARASYM In "Can the Subaltern Speak?" you argue that if the critique of the ideological subject constitution within state formation and systems of the "political economy" and if the "affirmative practice of the transformation of consciousness" are to be taken up, the shifting distinctions between representation as *Vertretung* (political representation) and as *Darstellung* must not be effaced. Could you elaborate on this distinction and indicate what place the double session of representation occupies within your work on the gendered subject?

SPIVAK First, about *Vertretung*, stepping in someone's place, really. *Tritt* (from *treten*, the second half of *vertretung*) has the English cognate *tread*. So that it might make it easier to look at this word as a word. *Vertretung*, to tread in someone's shoes, represents that way. Your congressional person, if you are talking about the United States, actually puts on your shoes when he or she represents you. Treading in your shoes, wearing your shoes, that's *Vertretung*. Representation in that sense: political representation. *Darstellung*—*Dar*, there, same cognate. *Stellen*, is to place, so "placing there." *Representing*: proxy and portrait, as I said, these are two ways of representing. Now, the thing to remember is that in the act of representing politically, you actually represent yourself and your constituency in the portrait sense, as well. You have to think of your constituency as working class, or the black minority, the rainbow coalition, or yet the military-industrial complex and so on. That is representation in the sense of *Darstellung*. So that you do not ever "simply" *vertreten* anyone, in fact, not just politically in the sense of true parliamentary forms, but even in political practices outside of parliamentary forms. When I speak as a feminist, I'm representing, in the sense of *Darstellung*, myself because we all know the problems attendant even upon defining the subject as a sovereign deliberative consciousness. But then if you take the sovereign deliberate consciousness and give it an adjective like feminist, that is, in fact, a rather narrow sense of self-representation, which you cannot avoid. But, what I'm saying is that this shifting line between treading in the shoes of all the disenfranchised women in my corner, and if I were very hubristic I would say, in the world. That way of representing: I speak for them and represent them. *Darstelling* them, portraying them as constituencies of feminism, myself as a feminist. Unless the complicity between these two things is kept in mind, there can be a great deal of political harm. The debate between essentialism and anti-essentialism is really not the crucial debate. It is not possible to be non-essentialist, as I said; the subject is always centered. The real debate is between these two ways of representing. Even non-fundamentalist philosophies must represent themselves as non-foundationalist philosophies. For example, you represent yourself when you speak *as* a deconstructor. There's the play between these two kinds of representations. And that's a much more interesting thing to keep in mind than always to say, "I will not be an essentialist."

I heard when I went to Alabama to listen to Derrida talking on Kant, that apparently in the morning—and I was unable to be present at the session in the morning—the speaker had referred to an expression of mine in that *Thesis Eleven*[18] interview, "strategic use of essentialism." Hillis Miller actually told me this, and he said, "Well, you know people talked about you and it was stressed that Stephen Heath had actually said this before you and that you had learned it from Stephen Heath." I said, "Well, I might have but not through reading the text. I don't know how then. I thought that I was thinking about this myself but who knows." Then he said that the point was made that you had said that feminists have to be strategic essentialists. I said, "Well, since I wasn't there, I don't know what was actually said. But I, myself, had thought I was saying that since it is not possible not to be an essentialist, one can self-consciously use this irreducible moment of essentialism as part of one's strategy. This can be used as part of a "good" strategy as well as a "bad" strategy and this can be used self-consciously as well as unself-consciously, and neither self-consciousness nor unself-consciousness can be valorized in my book. As for Stephen Heath, I don't know. The relationship between the two kinds of representation brings in, also, the use of essentialism because no representation can take place—no *Vertretung*, representation—can take place without essentialism. What it has to take into account is that the "essence" that is being represented is a representation of the other kind, *Darstellung*. So that's the format, right, and I think I've already said enough about the format to show how this would apply to representing the gendered subject also.

One last word. The reason why I am so devoted to the fiction of Mahasweta Devi is because she is very careful about—and now since we are talking about literary technique, our terms take on a slightly different meaning—she is very careful about representing the gendered, subaltern as she represents her. So that single-issue bourgeois feminists, who want to represent themselves as *the* people—I'm now quoting Marx on the typical gesture of the petit bourgeoisie when they want themselves to be understood as *the* people, so that the "real" people can take short shrift; they are very irritated about the fact that Mahasweta Devi doesn't do this herself, and speak *as* the gendered subaltern *herself*. But the strength of her texts is that this shifting play between the two kinds of representation is always intact there in various ways. That is what gives them their difficulty and that's what gives them their power.

HARASYM   When you were lecturing in Alberta you argued that Marxism, feminism and deconstruction must critically interrupt each other. Could you comment on this program?

SPIVAK   O.K., my notion of interruption. I kind of locate myself in that idea as a place of the reinscription of the dialectic into deconstruction. It's already there—interruption. My example is, always, Marx's discussion of industrial capitalism in *Capital*, Vol. 2, when he talks about the three moments of industrial capitalism interrupting each other, but, thus, providing a single circuit. He is using—it so happens that the example he is using is ambiguous. Industrial capitalism is not an unquestioned good in Marx, to say the least. But, on the other hand, if one reads Marx carefully, there is also the relationship between what Marx called *Vergesellschaftet* labor, which is translated as "associated labor" in English, but it's not a very happy translation because *Vergesellschaftet* is a very awkward and clumsy word; whereas, associated labor is a common word which makes us think about various workers' associations and so on. But anyway, what Marx calls *Vergellschaftet* labor in his work learns a lot morphologically from what happens in the moment of industrial capitalism. This, unfortunately, has been narrativized into "One must pass through advanced capitalism in order to get to socialism." I can't talk about that in the interview because we are focusing on something else. But, to go back to industrial capitalism, its place is dubious. But, nonetheless, this morphological articulation of a necessary interruption which allows something to function is very interesting, and, just as I said in terms of the politics of the open end and the great-narrative politics in the same way, it seems to me, that Marxism which focuses and must focus in order to be useful (a) on labor that is productive of self-valorizing value and the problems of disguising that situation, and how, to use

Marx's own words, how to read the proper signification of that scenario through the language of commodities, *Warensprache*, on the other hand, and feminism, on the other, is one of interruption. Feminism, must think of the human being predicated as work in senses other than this definition of the work that produces self-valorizing value. Feminism is involved with both anti-sexist work and transformation of consciousness outside of the Marxist project, which is to make the worker his (or her) unwitting production of capitalism. And deconstruction which is the critical moment, the reminder of catachresis, the reminder of the politics of the open end, or of the politics of great-narrative, depending on what the moment asks for, the reminder of the fact that any really "loving" political practice must fall a prey to its own critique. This reminder is, also, and necessarily, an interruption of both of these projects.

Unless there is this understanding, there will be divisiveness in the radical camp. Crisis management in the global economy will, in fact, act according to these productive interruptions, and we, on the other side, like stupid fools will take the interruptions as divisive positions so we are at each other's throats.

And, of course, the historian and the teacher of literature is a small example, a small case, if you like, of what happens when disciplinary privileging makes us forget that we can pull together even if we bring each other in crisis. One of the great cases was E.P. Thompson and Althusser, in *The Poverty of Philosophy*.[19] Another case now is Habermas' completely useless task of deriding Derrida. Habermas makes a lot of sense in the history of the West German political context. He makes a mistake by universalizing it. He also makes a mistake by confronting Derrida, whose project is quite discontinuous with his. How does he do it? By trivializing and canonizing a kind of disciplinary subdivision of labor, in his latest essay, *The Philosophical Discourse of Modernism*,[20] where he chides Derrida because Derrida is not honoring the disciplinary prerogatives of philosophy and literature as they have developed in the European academy since the eighteenth century. And Habermas gives to rhetoric a completely trivializing definition as literary style, as it were, and in the interest of this kind of honoring of disciplinary subdivision of labor, which is quite useful up to a point, he throws away anything which might be useful in deconstruction. Just as I said, it's not a matter of throwing away one and keeping the other but bringing the two to productive crisis. You see these examples where one is privileged so that all you have is division—people can't work together anyway; whereas, on the other side, what wins is precisely people pulling together. That's my last word. Thank you.

HARASYM   Thank you.

Notes

1. Gayatri Chakravorty Spivak, *In Other Worlds: Essays in Cultural Politics* (New York: Methuen, 1987), p. 221.

2. Gayatri Chakravorty Spivak, *Myself I Must Remake: The Life and Poetry of W.B. Yeats* (New York: Crowell, 1974).

3. Jacques Derrida, *Of Grammatology*, trans. Gayatri Chakravorty Spivak (Baltimore: John Hopkins University Press, 1976).

4. Gayatri Chakravorty Spivak, "Can the Subaltern Speak?" in *Marxism and the Interpretation of Culture* ed. Cary Nelson and Lawrence Grossberg (Urbana & Chicago: University of Illinois Press, 1988), pp. 271–313.

5. Spivak, *In Other Words*, pp. 154–78.

6. *Social Text* 15 (Fall 1986): 3–54.

7. See, for example, Spivak, "Feminism and Critical Theory," *In Other Worlds*, pp. 77–92.

8. Jacques Derrida, *Otobiographies: L'enseignement de Nietzsche et la politique du nom propre* (Paris: Galilée, 1984); *The Ear of the Other: Otobiography Transference, Translation*, trans. Peggy Kamuf (New York: Schocken Books, 1985).

9. Jacques Derrida, "Geschlect—différence sexuelle, différence ontologique," *Research in Phenomenology 13* (1983), 68–84.

10. Teresa Brennan, *Between Feminism and Psychoanalysis* (New York: Routledge, 1989).

11. Perry Anderson, *In the Tracks of Historical Materialism* (Chicago: University of Chicago Press, 1984).

12. Mahasweta Devi, "Breast-Giver", trans. Gayatri Chakravorty Spivak, *In Other Worlds*, pp. 222–40.

13. Jacques Derrida, "D'un ton apocalyptique: Adopté naguère en philosophie," *Les fins de l'homme à partir du travail de Jacques Derrida* (Paris: Galilée, 1981), pp. 445–86; Of an Apocalyptique Tone Recently Adopted in Philosophy," trans. John P. Leavey, Jr., *Semeia* 25 (1982): 63–96.

14. Jacques Derrida, *La voix et le Phénomène* (Paris: Presses Universitaires de France, 1967); *Speech and Phenomena and Other Essays on Husserl's Theory of Signs*, trans. D. Allison (Evanston: Northwestern University Press, 1973), pp. 3–88.

15. Gayatri Chakravorty Spivak, "Imperialism and Sexual Difference," *Oxford Literary Review* 8, no. 1–2 (1986): 225–40.

16. Paul de Man, *Allegories of Reading-Figural Language in Rousseau, Nietzsche, Rilke, and Proust* (New Haven and London: Yale University Press, 1979).

17. Wlad Godzich, "Introduction: Caution! Reader at Work!" in Paul de Man, *Blindness and Insight: Essays in the Rhetoric of Contemporary Criticism* (Minneapolis: University of Minnesota Press, 1983), pp. xxiv–xxix.

18. Gayatri Chakravorty Spivak, "Criticism, Feminism and the Institution," *Thesis Eleven* 10/11 (1984–85): 175–87.

19. Thompson, *The Poverty of Philosophy* (London: Merlin, 1978).

20. Habermas, *The Philosophical Discourse of Modernism* (Cambridge: MIT Press, 1987).

9

The *Intervention* Interview

First published in the Southern Humanities Review, Fall 1988, *the following interview with Gayatri Spivak was secured by Terry Threadgold, Department of English, and Peter Hutchings of the Intervention Collective, both of the University of Sydney, Australia. The occasion was the 1985 Cultural Construction of Race Conference in Sydney, which Professor Spivak attended as a guest speaker. The questions posed in the interview, though inspired by the conference, were delivered in writing after the conference and read, in the interests of recreating the situation of an interview, by Frances Bartkowski of Wesleyan University.*

FRAN   I have tried to combine here the questions which were suggested to me by the editors of *Intervention* with some of my own. They all focus on your presence in Australia as guest speaker at the Cultural Construction of Race Conference, on issues raised in your talk at that conference or in the panel discussion at the end of it. You are seen by others to occupy a number of different roles within the international context in which you speak and work. Third World woman, high-ranking U. S. academic woman, internationally known and invited guest speaker, and so on. These roles position you in a number of historically and ideologically specific and to some extent conflicting ways. This seems to be related to the question of the historical production of subjectivity, "the history against which the individual finds a place in social structure," which Phil Barker's paper* brought up yesterday and which you have yourself been concerned with in recent work. Would you like to comment on your current intellectual and political position in these terms?

GAYATRI   This is a question about roles. It's interesting that the "I" in the question which Fran made her own is actually Terry Threadgold, and the yesterday in the question now is no longer yesterday. We are speaking on the 20th August, 1985, in Middletown, Connecticut. To go back to the quotation from Phil's talk, my own feeling is that one works

---

*See Marie de Lepervanche and Gillian Bottomley, eds. *The Cultural Construction of Race* (Series: Sydney Studies in Society and Culture, no. 4 [Sydney, Australia, 1988]), p. 132 ff. The paper is entitled, "'My Struggle': The Congealing History."

with history as much as against it, taking history to be something like a script that is at one's command as an assignment. That is an assumption one must make as one moves. You have given me some labels that are put on me. They belong to related but different scripts of history. I think, offhand I would say, that I try to *do*, or I find myself doing, different things with the different labels. The first one that you have given is Third World woman. I think with that title I try to show why perhaps it is not all right to have such a portmanteau description of someone who was born in Calcutta in the '40s in a metropolitan professional middle-class family. The idea of the Third World as a monolithic entity comes out of a new organization of the international division of labor after the Second World War, and we who are from the other side of the globe very much fight against the labelling of all of us under that one rubric, which follows from the logic of neo-colonialism. So, with that one label I try to show my students and my audiences, why it actually reflects the site of a desire for people in the First World (now I'm using the counter-label) to have a manageable other.

As for being a senior academic in the United States, I try to use the advantages that come to me with that sort of positioning for the tenuring and advancement of younger folk who are doing radical criticism in their own way and who find the senior people at their own institutions generally not in sympathy with them. This involves a lot of just humdrum labor—reading lots of manuscripts, writing lots of tenure reviews, sitting on National Organization Fellowship Committees, and so on. I try not to refuse these things, because it seems to me that those of us who are in senior positions doing radical critique should in fact not turn their backs on this responsibility. But I'd also like to say as a kind of personal aside that whatever the seniority, or to use your word "high rank," looks like from the outside, in fact I do not belong to the closed top level of the United States academy. I have taught so far only at large state universities in the Middle West (in Iowa) and in the Southwest (in Texas), and now I teach at a small private school in the South (in Georgia), and perhaps you might know that the actual cultural elite in the United States inhabit the Northeastern seaboard or the West Coast. [Professor Spivak is currently Andrew W. Mellon Professor of English at the University of Pittsburgh.] So here, too, in a much lighter vein, I would like to say that "high-ranking U. S. academic" is not as much of a monolithic description as you think, although the case is not at all as serious as the label "Third World woman." Also I find it useful to look at the challenge posed by teaching the Superpower. I teach freshman composition and sophomore literature by choice because it seems to me that when one confronts young people in a country such as the United States today the politics of pedagogy become very clear. I think since the question is long I'll close this one right here, by saying that all of this comes accompanied by large doses of liberal guilt about which I do not know what to begin to say, but I'm sure you understand what the problem is.

Now let's look at the script of the internationally invited guest speaker. I'm a little diffident about the fact that I'm getting to be such a demagogue. I consider that a bit of a problem. My students know this very well because my classrooms become a place of active self-criticism of this demagogic manner, so we work with it and against it (*not* by self-flagellation). Having said that, let me confess that I consider it an incredible stroke of good fortune, really, to be able to interact with these very different kinds of audiences all over the world. As far as I'm concerned it has been a highly educative experience, because it makes you realize how provincial the discourses of various identifiable arenas are in the global context. When you speak in the United States, and you speak in Britain, and you speak in Australia, speak in India, speak in Hong Kong, speak in Africa, speak in Cairo, speak in Saudi Arabia, you begin to realize that the incredible arrogance of an arena that takes itself to be the world is something that one must undermine persistently all the time. It's been very educative for me. I think in this context I also try to explain, and use, the phenomenon of tokenization. You use just a few of the labels, Third World woman, U. S. academic, but there are also labels that are used in a tokenizing way, Marxist, deconstructivist, feminist, and so on, and I try actually to bring that phenomenon into my discourse so that the whole circuit of international conferences and lectures to an extent becomes my subject matter; that's how I use it. Although I'm a little bit unsure about my control over this particular thematic, I still am so dazzled by the fact that for one reason or another I seem to be travelling a great deal these days. I can't speak with as much control about it as I can about my political concerns, about Third World-ism or about my status in the United States since I have been teaching for twenty years.

I'd like to say a couple more things in answer to this question. The script of being a Indian without nationalism and being a Bengali without regionalism is the one that poses the greatest problem for me. I am trying to win back, to relearn how to be these things again. In a Bengali context, what I have to think about a lot is not just left politics, or academic behavior, but about my various kinship inscriptions within India, not just in my family, but in the way in which a society like the Indian society perceives a woman's public presence in terms of kinship inscriptions of mother, sister, daughter, even aunt. How can I insert myself, how can I inscribe myself within a culture—"my own"—which actually looks at men and women in public in terms of these kinship inscriptions? The whole business of Indira Gandhi being mother was not just an international press hype. There *is* a certain way in which kinship, the discourse of the family, rather than the discourse of the state, is *active* in the Indian or the Bengali context, certainly of my class, and I'm trying to learn that one, instead of looking at it from the outside, because I belong in it. In the direct kinship context, for example, when there are weddings in the family, I discovered, after my marriages broke up, and I became of a certain age, that when the bride or the groom was blessed, I have to step out of the room, because I'm the mark of bad luck, as a married woman without a husband; now that's a kind of kinship inscription as well, and it's no use actually taking an adversative position in that context because, on the other side, it's also true that in the so-called "developed," feminist countries, like the United States, my credit in the heterosexist commoditied marketplace is very low because I'm an intellectual woman, past her first youth, so one has somehow to work the dialectic between these two things, and for me, these roles are much more *immediately* politically problematic than the ones you have mentioned. I find now that my work is coalescing around strange single female figures like the Rani of Sirmur (about whom I spoke last year at Griffith). I can't get a grip on them. Like Bhuvaneswari Bhaduri, the young woman who killed herself, about whom I also spoke in Australia last year. I can't quite get a grip on her. And then there are other women of whom I could speak—and it seems to me that when I look at these women and how difficult it is to construct them as objects of investigation, that relates, with this whole business of Indian-ness and Bengali-ness, much more intrinsically than all the *big* labels like U. S. academic or Third World woman or international star. O. K. I'm going to wind this question down now so perhaps the very last thing I will say is that, all in all, all of these few roles that I've spoken of in the long run help me in the discovery of the discontinuities between my two deepest concerns, Marxism and feminism.

FRAN   Before I go on to the next question, would you care to say what you *would* put in the place of roles?

GAYATRI   I don't know what I would put in the place of roles. I think I balked slightly at the word "roles" because it brings in the opposition between sincerity and having to pretend. I think the word "inscription" is—for me—a good . . . sort of *hypothèse de travail*, what's the word . . . working hypothesis or something—assumption, because it seems to me if one sees these social texts, various social texts, U. S. academy—international division of labor—as putting one in a certain, large writable context, as it were, one could say that one is "inscribed"—as one thing or another—so I find the alternate metaphor perhaps would be "inscription" rather than "role-playing"—you know—I write myself as I am written as it were, but "script" after all is a word that is very close to "roles" isn't it? So there you are. . . .

FRAN   The second question is a run-on from the last one and comes from *Intervention*. "We perceive the fact of your growing celebrity as something you use as a political praxis—would you be willing to accept this view and what difficulties do you have with it?"

GAYATRI   Well, you know, the "growing celebrity" is—I can't really deal with it except as a kind of a joke, but I think I have answered some of it already in the first question, but I think that the part of my "grand celebrity" that I like most is the surprise it brings me at the good reading that people seem to be giving to my texts—it makes me much more careful about what I write, and what I say, because that whole feeling of freedom to speak has, I think, taken on a kind of corrective aura, now that I see that there are good minds, concerned minds, that are actually paying a good deal of attention to my prose. I think that's how it's affected my political praxis of the production of discourse, because that's the arena where it works.

FRAN   O. K. I've a little trouble here reading this question.

GAYATRI   Shall I have a look at it?

FRAN   Yes, perhaps you should—there's someone's name here that I'm not sure of—right. The name is Marie de Lepervanche. *That,* I think— is "greatest radical." Terry Threadgold's handwriting or script is causing us some amusement here. These questions are concerned with your position regarding feminism. A comment that was made by Marie de Lepervanche on a panel discussion yesterday—was the quote "Women are subject to ideological 'slippage'—pushed around by men." An accurate description in the context in which she was talking. But you have spoken against a too-simplistic approach to the quote "Women are oppressed by male power" question in many ways that are contrary to some hard-line feminist positions. Yesterday, you spoke also of literary criticism and of feminism as one of its greatest radical potentials. I wonder if you could talk about these issues in relation to the questions suggested by *Intervention*. And, this is the question from *Intervention*: "Some feminists have expressed surprise at your continued public enthusiasm for feminism. You also talk about 'hard' feminism. What do you mean by this?"

GAYATRI   I don't have any problems with starting from the position that "Women are universally oppressed by men." I think that in order to start your practice, you have to have some kind of provisional starting point, and I think that's fine, but when it becomes a door-closer, that's when I begin to have trouble. It's a very simple point, really. I mean perhaps that it's true that on *every* class level you have male oppression of females; it's also true that one can't shift classes just at will, so that the male of a very much lower class is not immediately an oppressor of a female of a very much higher class or race. If one is aware of the other struggles, that awareness cleanses the kind of monolithic assumption that we are speaking for all women's oppression. I've often made the point that in the United States, when female academics involved in tenure struggle, which is quite often the only really political activity they are fully engaged in, use the excuse of women's universal oppression, they are certainly not thinking about women in the Bantustans, or of the urban sub-proletariat in Hong Kong. They are not thinking of unorganized peasant labor in India. Because in fact in their tenure struggle every day, they do things that make the position of these three groups that I have mentioned, worse; and they are themselves not even aware that that is so.* In the absence of that awareness, to bring up women's universal oppression as an excuse when you quite correctly want a more solid situation in your workplace—seems little more than an excuse—which doesn't mean that I'm not against sexism every way, all the time, every day—these two issues are quite different. I should say that I always find single-issue movements frightening. In fact, the extreme piety with which Communist parties insist that everything *must* be explained in terms of class struggle and the mode of production narrative also gives me a great deal of anxiety. The historical work that I'm engaged in, the inscription of Indian/colonial history from the point of view of peasant insurgency, encounters a lot of opposition from party-line communism—communist explanations around the world, because of the so-called pre-political position of the peasant, its non-accession to the class struggle, etc. This to me is a kind of parallel example to the absolute insistence on women's oppression being the final determinant of any problem that one is considering. So it's really from that angle that I find feminism as a single-issue movement somewhat terrifying because it leads to the totalizing that all great narrative explanations finally bring us face to face with. And as someone interested in deconstruction I'm deeply concerned with a persistent critique of a totalization which can in fact in the long run lead to totalitarianism.

I was speaking of feminism as the movement with the greatest radical potential within literary criticism. Literary criticism is basically a Western discipline with a very specific subject. Given the kinds of institutions within which literary criticism flourishes, I feel that if feminism did not go exactly the line that it was going today, then it does have the potential of opening up the discipline in various, *most* interesting ways. That's where my hope and confidence lie. I wasn't speaking of the globe, I was

---

*See "Feminism and Critical Theory," in Gayatri Spivak, *In Other Worlds. Essays in Cultural Politics* (New York and London: Methuen, 1987), 77-92.

speaking of my workplace within which my practice operates. If I were sitting with you now, I would have asked, "*What* feminists?"—when you say *some* feminists have expressed surprise—feminists also come in various stripes and colors—and then I would have asked, "Why do you say 'my continued *public* enthusiasm for feminism'?" Is there any reason to suspect that in my private conduct I am not that enthusiastic about feminism, that it's the *line* I feel I should take in public? Is there something implicit there? And then I would ask *why* the word "enthusiasm" is being used there. The question itself seems to me to have various problems. But failing that, since I can't settle that with you in a conversation, I would repeat myself, and I would say that since I am most interested in collective power, that is the collective to which I have the greatest "safe" access. I live in the United States as a resident alien with hardly any civil rights, and I live in a country where there is no Indian labor force, so that I'm not the direct object of racism as I would be in Britain, so that the feminist collective—given my job—in fact, that's not just within the academy either, in the union movement, in other kinds of social movements, the feminist collective is the one to which I have the safest access. And therefore, in fact, what I express, not only in public, but also in private, and not only enthusiastically, but also practically, is *that* sentiment that you hear. As for high feminism, I don't think I need to explain what I mean. In a very brief sentence, I consider that high feminism where highly privileged women see their face in the mirror and define "Woman"—capital *w*—in terms of the reflection that they see there: sometimes they look at their face, sometimes they look at their genitals, and in terms of that, they adjudicate about woman as such. I have very little patience with that. I think that perhaps we should go on to the next question.

FRAN   Is that the kind of thing that you have in mind when you say that academic women, when they are involved in their own struggles, might worsen the situations of those three groups that you mentioned? What would you have them—what would you like to see them do that might be different from the . . .

GAYATRI   Well, you know—no—that's not the group that I was thinking about. That group, you know the people who, working for themselves, actually shaft people elsewhere—I see them as in fact reproducing the structures of the patriarchal societies of which they are a product. O.K.? By high feminism I mean the kind of ethereal feminist theory where the female sexed subject is constantly theorized in terms of psychoanalysis and counter-psychoanalysis simply in terms of absences in texts and so on, and so forth, et cetera, where really what I hear is the history of the last 300 years in the intellectual arena in the West. That's what I was thinking of. What goes by the name of capital *t* Theory within feminism. That's what I call high feminism.

FRAN O. K., the next question goes like this (from *Intervention*): "Analysis almost always ends us at a textual level. We start and tend to end with a text upon which we have passed some judgement. In your practice, is there any way to get beyond this?" And then Threadgold says, "This is surely related to your reference to Benjamin on the panel yesterday, and to the question of what he calls 'reconstellation,' and there the xeroxing has cut off what Gayatri remembers as a rather interesting question in the first draft of these questions that she managed to lose."

GAYATRI I'm a bit puzzled by that question. Because it seems to rest on a kind of artificial pre-critical opposition between the verbal text (which is what is meant by text: reading books and so on) and the picket line. There are books, and then there is practice. So I can't really answer it in the same theoretical vein in which I tackled the others. If you want to know how to become an activist, there are the usual kinds of answers. You look out to see what kinds of demonstrations are going on, you read the newspapers, if you see something is happening which is clearly against social justice and nothing has been organized there, you try to organize, you look at how resistances are developing in terms of clear cases of social injustice, etc., you join the demonstrations, you join groups, etc., etc. That's how one becomes an activist, I mean, to escape the text as you understand it—the verbal text. There are these various ways, in which you become "involved." But, once you do that you won't get away from textuality. "The Text," in the sense we use it, is not just books. It refers to the possibility that every socio-political, psycho-sexual phenomenon is organized by, woven by many, many strands that are discontinuous, that come from way off, that carry their histories within them, and that are not within our control. We are inserted in them, as I said, in answer to your first question. If you get totally involved in political activism, you will find that you become more and more aware of the problems of the textuality of the socius. You will not go away from the text by deciding to join movements, or by deciding to stop reading books. A bullet in the chest, the fact of the death, might seem to stop textuality, but the reason why the bullet, the access to the bullet, why the bullet at all; who killed whom, why, how? Why without reason, etc.? All of these, in fact, if we are going to do anything about it, rather than simply advance it as an example of where the text stops—if we are going to *do* anything about the phenomenon, we have *no* alterative but to involve ourselves and mire ourselves in what we are calling the textuality of the socius. The real task here is to displace and undo that killing opposition between the text narrowly conceived as the verbal text and activism narrowly conceived as some sort of mindless engagement. I think that's about as much as I can say in *this* context about the question.

I'm very sorry that the bit on reconstellation got cut off, but I think I'd better not try answering a question that's not there. Now then, hang on a second, why don't we just substitute other words?

FRAN   To return to your talk at the conference—and to some of the issues: you mentioned that many of the attempts to deal with racism at the conference had maintained racism as the object of investigation. Would you like to speak about the sense in which you see the politicization of deconstruction as a way of overcoming this subject/object dichotomy?

GAYATRI   Well, there's a great deal to say here but, *pour faire vite,* I will mention the part of deconstruction that I found useful for the talk at the conference, since I saw such a clear opposition being set up, unwittingly, between the subjects of investigation—the people who were speaking at the conference—and the *two* objects of investigation, that is to say, the subject of race and the subject of the racist. I felt that that opposition had to be deconstructed in some way, and the way for me was—a way which is crucial; everything I've said so far in fact has related to that—to fix on that one presupposition of deconstruction which problematizes the positionality of the subject of investigation. If you talk about the class struggle—the mode of production narrative—as the final determinant, or if you speak about women's oppression as the final determinant, you take a stand, distinguishing yourself from capitalists, racists, men, and also, of course, from the people of the other races, you are, to an extent, making yourself, as the *subject* of investigation, transparent, and deconstruction will not allow this. You're not just invisible but transparent, which is much worse. Through you one can see the problem without any interference, and this is a very serious claim. It is a serious questioning of the sovereignty of the subject, it's not just breast-beating. As I said in my talk, the sort of breast-beating which stops the possibility of social change is to say, "I'm only a white male, I cannot speak as a feminist," or, "I'm only a white male and cannot speak for the blacks." You know that whole thing about "Oh, there was no voice of the other because there were no black anthropologists here," et cetera. What we are asking for is that the hegemonic discourses, the holders of hegemonic discourse should de-hegemonize their position and themselves learn how to occupy the subject position of the other rather than simply say, "O. K., sorry, we are just very good white people, therefore we do not speak for the blacks." That's the kind of breast-beating that is left behind at the threshold and then business goes on as usual. The deconstructive problemization of the positionality of the subject of inves tigation has stood me in very good stead. That is what was reflected when I refused marginalization when there were questions from the floor about my practice and so on. One of the things I said was that one of my projects is not to allow myself to occupy the place of the marginal that you would like to see me in, because then that allows you to feel that you have an other to speak to. That comes from that deconstructive move. In this sense, to go back to my first answer, deconstruction gives a certain critical edge to all possible totalizations of this kind. The structure of complicity, why we should be *there,* why they should be *here,* what is getting lost—those are the kinds of things that deconstructive investigation of this area allows you to look at: the ways in which you are complicit with what you are so carefully and cleanly opposing. That leads to much better practice in my view. It seems to me that the understanding of deconstruction as leading to paralysis is to see it merely as a negative metaphysics which would like to be completely anti-essentialist (as if that were possible). Negative metaphysics leads not to paralysis on the part of people who are privileged enough to repudiate essentialism, et cetera. It leads, to use a very old-fashioned word, to irresponsibility, self-congratulation, and fun for some people. The view of deconstruction that I'm proposing here keeps it very clear from (excuse me for fabulating historically) the massive reaction to the failure of 1848 in Europe which brought with it a certain kind of negative metaphysics.

I'm getting into very deep waters, and to mix metaphors, this is one of my hobby horses; I don't think you want to watch me riding my hobby horse across deep waters, so go on to the next one.

FRAN   O.K., I could ask a question but it might take you too far off the track, so I'll go on to the next question.

GAYATRI   Riding a hobby horse here across deep waters and going too far off the track! I hope you will keep this ridiculous conjuncture in your text.

FRAN   Could you expound on some of the comments you made on culture in your talk? You said for example that the use of culture in the conference title as the medium or agent of the construction of race involved both a metalepsis and a politics. Could you explain your use of these terms in particular?

GAYATRI   Well, I was using the word metalepsis to mean in a rather strict way the substitution of one figure for another. In this case I was talking about the substitution of cause and effect, cause for effect, effect for cause, and even a sort of confusion between cause and effect; I believe in fact Robert Miles also spoke about this in his own way. It seems, as I was saying—hang on a second, I'm going to stop the tape and get Franny a bit more comfortable. O.K., it seems to me that this culture, if culture is taken as an agent, as in "cultural construction of race," then what we tend to lose sight of is that culture is also something that is the effect of the production of cultural explanations, and cultural explanations are produced also because a certain culture needs to be fabricated, a monolithic explanation of a group needs to be fabricated. I'm not suggesting that there is nothing like culture. I'm suggesting that when it is taken as an agent and given a certain descriptive power describing groups generally outlined by nation state outlines, a certain politics of discursive production is going on there. It is a curious phenomenon that most culturalist explanations are given by people who want to dissimulate the question of ideology, who want to dissimulate that not everybody is the "custodian of culture" in the same way, in every "culture," that the word "culture" and the word "cultured" have connotations that have something like a relationship. This might hold *even* for studies of so-called mass culture, so-called popular culture. There are ways in which the political question is dissimulated there, because most popular culture, counter-culture, mass culture studies are ferociously nation-centered, and they are generally studies of national cultures. When we look at the word "culture" we should see it as the site of a struggle, a problem, a discursive production, an effect structure rather than a cause. Those are some of the reasons why I am dubious about the present trend of speaking about the cultural construction of gender and race. It would be rather difficult to speak about the cultural construction of class because class *is* the issue that gives the lie to notions of cultural construction of anything. Yet the way in which a pure class-struggle grid is sometimes imposed upon scenes of domination in the Third World could be "culturalist"! It should also be said, that sometimes in these high-minded arguments about the cultural construction of gender and race, implicitly, the heterogeneity of one's own culture is protected, because one sees oneself as outside of the cultural construction of gender and race or as a victim of it; whereas the homogeneity of other cultures is implicitly taken for granted. I have argued against this at length in my job. In the long run, you don't in fact talk about your own culture at all, although you do talk about other cultures as if they are homogeneous. For example, at this conference most of the talk that I heard was concerned about immigration laws. Now immigration laws are not your culture. On the other hand, when you are speaking about those against whom the laws were being perpetrated you had your feet firmly on the ground of their cultural identity. It seems to me that the politics involved in presupposing the heterogeneity of one's own, one's own separation from that cultural heritage and the homogeneity of the other is something that one should examine. Here I would like to point out a very enjoyable text that speaks about the risks of culturalism in the Afro-American context. It's a short story by Tone Cade Bambara called "My Man Bo-vanne." It's even to be found in the *Norton Anthology of American Litera-ture*. I would recommend a reading of that story to see how a militant black woman strikes against culturalism within the black movement in the United States.

FRAN   Shall we go on then to the next question, the rider to this question from Terry? I was interested in what you said on the panel (in reply to a question from Bruce Kapferer) about the difficulties of isolating racism as a problem, about the very attempt to do so being behind the times, since the whole concept of racism is being re-written. You said, "Sign systems are always fractured from the point of view of what is going on." We both know you are not a semiotician, but this seems to me to be an interesting way of putting what is a semiotic issue, and I wondered if you would like to elaborate on what you meant by it, or the other question of isolating racism.

GAYATRI   Well, isolating racism to an extent goes with my problem with single-issue movements. Isolating racism looks at the problem of race as having to do with people who want to come and settle in the so-called white countries, and that seems to me to be behind the times because it's a replay in reverse of an older cultural explanation. As I was saying the first day, there was a whole question during high colonialism of entitlement for us whites to live *there*, and now the critique of racism is entitlement of those niggers to live *here*, and it seems to me that that sort of two-step, you know, reversing cultural explanation, seems to be too simple in terms of "social realities." The reason why racism or anti-racism is used is because various ways of cultural self-representation *must* be used in the interest of political mobilization. On the right or on the left. There's nothing particularly wrong with that, of course—well, from the left—but, you see—and Terry, I'm very pleased that you at least went on record and said that I'm not a semiotician—I have the greatest embarrassment when people somehow make me a semiotician—and therefore, if I may do a little bit of home-grown semiotics . . . Something must be tapped when you are mobilizing, something must be tapped that makes political sense. What makes sense here comes from a color *system*, from an orderly instituted color system. As for the notion of fracture—I'm not saying that there *is* something out there from which the sign system that is already instituted lags behind. I'm saying that there is something like an irreducible lag-effect. You understand, it's not that you then must presume what is "behind" the sign-system or "after" it, which the system can't keep up with, as the "real thing"—but you must take into account that what you are tapping in terms of cultural self-representation in order to mobilize, or what you are noticing the other side as tapping, *also* in order to mobilize, must always work with this lag-effect, so that the real task of the political activist is persistently to undo the lag-effect—just as the task of the political activist may be to undo a metalepsis—to undo this lag-effect—this *Nachträglichkeit*—this irreducible *après-coup*. The place where political activism becomes critical is when it notices that the cultural self-representation, the slogans for mobilization, are, in fact, lagging behind—nothing perhaps—but they have the lagging-behind effect so that you don't take your slogan as adequately representing a reality. That's what you have to take into account, and, speaking as a political activist, that's what I was doing when I was saying that racism is behind the times as a slogan. So, I hope this doesn't sound too theoretically convoluted to you—because what you heard was a practical use of this theoretical understanding that I have about the fact that any sign-system that you tap in order to "make sense, " being already instituted (like language itself, you inherit it, you don't make it out of whole cloth), must be seen as having a lag-effect. In the 1960s, in response to U. S. spontaneism, for example, one would say, "Look, take into account the fact that language is instituted—you're not making it up." Today, one would say that in all of these monolithic explanations, racism or whatever, one must take into account that they're being used within an instituted sign system. What I did a minute ago was to show how our present use of it is simply a replay in reverse of a much older discourse that came itself as a displacement of a discourse that was older yet because, after all, this pursuit and establishment of self-constituting others is older than what we are looking at as racism or sexism or whatever.

FRAN There were a number of terms used in your paper which I would like to ask you to talk about some more. You made a distinction between foreclosure and exclusion and spoke of the production of the colonial subject in terms of the foreclosure of epistemic violence, chromatism and the foreclosure of the international division of labor.

Would you explain your use of these terms? The question is from Terry.

GAYATRI If you don't mind, I'm going to go back to my text here. Foreclosure—oh dear! Hang on, yes, all right! I said, "Foreclosure is a colloquial use of a word that comes to us courtesy of that Freud who is a rhetorician of the unconscious." O.K. ? And, I was using it to mean the interested denial of something. There is an "interest" at work in the denial. It is when you are denying something—for example, that business about culturalism denegating ideology—the interested denial of something that is present crucially and in excess. Exclusion is—that you know that someone is there, but you don't want to exclude him or her—

that's a different thing—but when you're vigorously denying something, because it is present in excess, that's what I'm calling foreclosure. Now, what were the two examples of foreclosure?

FRAN   Epistemic violence and chromatism.

GAYATRI   Right. I was suggesting that when you construct a kind of simple subject of race, you forget that within colonialism—and imperialism, and crucial to their development of the institutions of the law, the imposition of—in the case of India—certain European codes, of largely English common law as law as such over a legal structure of performance that was very different, the imposition of a completely different educational system—and various other mechanisms actually changed what Foucault has called an "épistème" and produced the subjects—even if they are not "educated" colonially in the way that you would recognize. This epistemic violence of the production of a different subject is ignored when the us and them division between the object of race and the subject of racism is made so clearly. In the structures of our disciplinary production of the discourse of anti-racism I found a replication of the same structures of epistemic violence. This is being foreclosed, of course, because it's crucially present in excess. We're using the same to say, "To see the problem of race simply in terms of skin color does not recognize that the only arena for that problem is the so-called white world, because you are focusing the problem in terms of blacks who want to enter and live in the white world, under racial laws in the white world." That obliges us to ignore the fact that in countries which are recognized as Third World countries, there is a great deal of oppression, class oppression, sex oppression, going on in terms of the collusion between comprador capitalists and that very white world. The international division of labor does not operate in terms of good whites, bad whites, and blacks. A simple chromatism obliges you to be blind to this particular issue because once again it's present in excess. I was trying to show how our lives, even as we produce this chromatist discourse of anti-racism, are being constructed by that international division of labor, and its latest manifestations were in fact the responsibility of class-differentiated nonwhite people in the Third World, using the indigenous structures of patriarchy and the established structures of capitalism. To simply foreclose or ignore the international division of labor because that's complicit with our own production, in the interests of the black-white division as representing the problem, is a foreclosure of neo-colonialism operated by chromatist race-analysis.

FRAN   From *Intervention*:

"Australians are usually obsessed with being (a) in the provinces and (b) part of the global village. Is this a contradiction and/or a mythology, and what if any is the distinction between being a colony and a province of something?"

GAYATRI   Well, I don't know where the notion of global village comes from—I mean, of course I know about Marshall McLuhan and so on, but how it fits into this province/colony distinction. I think the way in which McLuhan spoke about global village operated the same kind of foreclosure of the international division of labor that I've been speaking of and is now being continued in the discourse of postmodernism as a universal discourse of "our time." The feudalization of the periphery, to use the Samir Amin's phrase, or the way in which the urban proletariat in Third World countries is supporting the production of postmodernism or the production of the global village in days of yore is simply ignored when that is taken—those kinds of lines of communication that exist all over the globe—supposedly are taken as describing the entire globe. So Australia to an extent is as much part of the global village as any country is, but it is, as I have been suggesting, not only class-differentiated but also differentiated in terms of which side of the international division of labor you inhabit. The international division of labor is not just between the First World and the Third World, as I was trying to say in my critique of chromatism in the last answer. Let's put that aside. As for the question of being a province or a colony you ask if that is in contradiction with being part of the global village. I don't think so. I think the same political impulse, or related political impulses are behind the claim to be part of the global village and the acknowledgement of the superiority of the First World as the metropolis, as it were. As for contradictions, as a Marxist I'm not afraid of them. There is indeed a certain kind of contradiction since related political impulses lead to both of these claims. There is a certain kind of contradiction in being in partnership with Japan, for example, in the Asia/Pacific as it is, and then the sort of feeling of intellectual suburbanism, or as you say, provincialism or being a colony, there is a certain kind of contradiction there which also shows us the gap between intellectual capital and capital as such in today's world, between the older slogan of "Knowledge is power," which is, which has, that lag-effect in terms of which Australia feels a province; and the rising hegemony of information control, which has nothing to do with being the subject of *knowledge* as such. I spoke of that in my talk, and I will not expatiate on it. But at any rate, I don't have a problem with something being a contradiction. I think contradictions can be productive. I don't know if you are using the word mythology as if there is some unadulterated truth somewhere which can be recovered and a myth which is in opposition to truth. I can't work with that particular distinction. I would ask the simple questions that I have been asking all through this conversation. What do you mean when you say Australian? Who are you? So that you know a person with my political convictions before I make those generalizations, those are the two questions I would ask myself. Who are Americans? Who are Indians? Who am I? Where am I in that context as I posed the question? What is the interest implicit in posing the question in that way? The identification with Anglo-Europe/U. S., so the situation of dominance against which Australia feels a province, only comes through a certain kind of identification. This was the subject of the conference. Who identifies in Australia with Anglo-Europe/U. S.? You in your question seem to think that that's how Australians should be described. Why is that particular problem not spoken of in the question? This is where I would fix my glance. That in fact, you, Terry, say in introducing the question that it focusses on Australia or Asia, perhaps because you read the question symptomatically, but as I look at the question I don't see Asia in it. From that point of view, too, I would have a problem. I've been thinking of the general ignoring of Asia that I saw in the conference; I'm quite sure that's not the case all over the Australian academy. But the word Asian was generally taken as a label constructed by Australian racism. I was musing all through these days, on the so-called ten Austro-Asiatic tribes in India. They are the object of all kinds of racism within the Indian subcontinent, and they are supposed to be Austro-Asiatic! The absence of Asia in this question, Terry's noticing, Terry's description of it as having to do with Australia and Asia, the definition of Australia in it—these are problems around which I would circle, rather than trying to diagnose a contradiction or a mythology where the word is used as in simple opposition to the way things really are, some sort of truth. As for colony and province, I think to look at the difference between words cne goes to the dictionary. Now Fran and I are in the library of the Center for the Humanities. I will just simply look at what the book says. This is the *OED*. The province is an extraordinarily interesting entry which goes for one, two, three, four, five, six, seven columns. The word is of uncertain derivation. That which offers at first sight—that is to say to conquer—*pro-* and then *vincere* does not explain the earliest known use in Latin, and so we start talking about provinces on the basis of a false etymology and a lost origin and being governed from outside Italy under Roman domination and administered by a governor sent from Rome. But the way it began to be understood was the administrative division of a country or state. It is the administrative and territorial division of a country. From that point of view, if Australia considers it's a province, you would see that there is a certain kind of homogeneity or identification assumed with Anglo-U. S.-Europe, and of course I am suggesting that to say that is to define Australia as a certain Australia. Even so it feels "provincial." Now implicitly the notion comes in that the provinces—just as there's culture and being cultured—are "provincial" in terms of the culture that's produced in the capital. The intellectual provincialism that you think "Australia" feels would lead, by the logic of the metaphor, to this *ensemble*. The first use of "colony" that the *OED* cites if from "colon"—tiller, farmer, cultivator, planter, and from that, settler in a new country, so that to an extent the difference between civilization and culture where we honor the difference between cities and countries, the civilization relating to *civitas*, the city, and culture to agriculture, horticulture growing from nature. Almost the same difference as between colony and province. So that when you're talking about colonization you are talking about settling a place which was unsettled before, and that brings us to an issue that I've spoken of many times before: the assumption that when the colonizers come to a world, they encounter it as uninscribed earth upon which they write their inscriptions. From that sense when you use the word Australia you are speaking the language of the colonizer, because you have decided that the name of this place is Australia. In fact Australia has no *right* to ignore this, marginalize itself, and feel like a colony. When it calls itself Australia, and when it is defined as you are defining it, that particular segment in fact *is* the colonizer rather than the colonized. The feeling that it is a colony is a kind of self-congratulation, self-marginalization in the way in which the first feminists in the 19th century in Britain used to identify themselves with the slaves. They identified with the anti-slavery movement by comparing themselves to slaves, and that indeed was a kind of self-marginalization. If Australia is indeed the place that you are defining, it's *your* proper name, Australia. Then there is a distinct difference between thinking of itself as a province, and thinking of itself as a colony. I hope I've said enough to point up the way in which this difference operates.

FRAN   The next question is related to the issue of politicizing deconstruction and comes from *Intervention*. "Could you talk about the difficulties of using deconstruction strategy vis à vis Marxist theory for political practice and could you elaborate on the current Marxist work which may include some of these strategies."

GAYATRI   I think the real problem is of course using any theory for any practice. The incursion of deconstruction didn't particularly create the problem of using Marxist theory for practice, or indeed using any theory for practice. Deconstruction does try—and this has nothing to do with Marxism as such—to confront the way in which practice always norms theory. That's a much bigger issue, and I don't think that's the kind or question that you're asking, and we're both running slightly out of steam so I'll focus the question, I'll decide to read your question in a slightly more focussed way. You see, the real problem is that the group that deconstructs is generally not the group that operates as Marxists, and that is why all of these very "interested" questions about deconstruction and Marxism arise. It's understood as the negative metaphysicians and decadents on the one side and the activists engaged in the class struggle on the other. That's what the question boils down to. I think though the group that deconstructs to an extent is also dependent on the traditions of the Left in the United States, Britain, and France. In the United States there is no significant political left, and within that I think deconstructive theory has come to inhabit Marxist theory much more significantly. Eminent Marxist critics like Jameson or Eagleton, whatever they say in their writing, try to clue in deconstructive strategies into their understanding of Marxism. This has nothing to do with the political arena in the United States, where if you wanted to have a political party on the left it begins to look more and more like very slightly left-of-center social democracy. That's not what we are talking about here. In Britain with its entrenched tradition of academic radicalism, deconstruction is not particularly taking on much of a foothold. It *is* taking in the arena of literary criticism where it replicates many of the structures that literary criticism has set up in opposition to political practice within the English field. So that the kind of literary criticism that is seen as having some kind of political practice relates to a kind of—I don't know how to put it—a sort of academic populism. I cannot think of a better word with which one can associate two people who are diametrically opposed to each other in their actual academic stance—Raymond Williams and F. R. Leavis. If you think of Terry Eagleton's work today, it situates itself within that tradition of academic populism in spite of the earlier work on Althusser and Benjamin. Already in the Benjamin book we begin to see the way in which Eagleton is moving from "high theory" into what I'm calling a kind of "populist," colloquially pragmatist, picket-line tradition of engaged literary criticism. So I think that's a different kind of problem which has nothing to do with Marxism per se and deconstruction per se and of course in France, the situation of the Communist party and the Socialist party and the failure of the *programme commun* in 1978, the situation of Althusser within the Communist party and then edging out of the Communist party, all of this has a lot to do with the role of deconstruction in France. As good a political practice-watcher as Perry Anderson, who has nothing going for deconstruction, as his book *In the Tracks of Historical Materialism* is ample proof of—Anderson did say that the one school that in fact has not broken completely with Marxism in France is Derridean deconstruction, or in fact Derridean deconstruction is not a part of post-Marxism of which French theory is the greatest example. My first answer to that question has to do with established traditions in the three countries where deconstruction has its play. Then

I did have that little bit before where I said that the notion of practice norming theory is a very useful one, but that's not where your question was at. I think the most accessible example to you would be the work of Antonio Negri. I can't start talking about his work here, but I would direct your attention to him. In my own understanding the work of the group called Subaltern Studies, the group I was speaking of as rewriting the history of Indian colonial historiography from the point of view of peasant insurgency, is the most active example of deconstructive historiography that I have seen. I have written a long piece explaining this which will find its place in their fourth collection. Once again I can only point you in that direction to see a careful establishment of this particular argument. But the strategy is to see how deconstruction does operate, in texts, you know, when you read Plato, for example. Derrida reads Plato and shows how in fact there is a certain kind of deconstructive argument in Plato. De Man reads Rousseau. So from that point of view, I would say that in political, in actual political practice, although it's girdled around by discourses of centrism, in successful political practice, in fact what we call deconstructive principles, are in operation. That's a very long argument which I couldn't possibly make here, but if we get together again, if we have another discussion, I would be happy to talk to you about actual cases of political practice. One quick example which I will not expatiate upon would be the relationship between guerrilla movements and party-line explanations of guerrilla movements which were discounted because the movement did not make the right connection which at the moment would have been alliance with the progressive bourgeoisie, and the guerrillas made a mistake, et cetera. We have heard these arguments. Now if one went into the analysis of what was going on, it might be possible to look at these examples and see how what we call deconstructive principles (which is a contradiction in terms) are being covered over in these kinds of operations. Now, on the other hand, when these movements succeed and come to power, things start to freeze, national liberation movements quite often freeze internationalism. There the persistent critique within a deconstructive view would stand as a *momento mori,* so that the fact that those deconstructive practices were girdled around by discourses of centrism is where we would focus our glance. With great trepidation I would say that Marxism in fact is a critical philosophy. Its transformation into a substantive philosophy, a utopian philosophy that can be adequately represented by revolution and social reform has been in fact a centrist mistake. To go far beyond the scope of your question, let me say that in order to stop being Marxist fundamentalists and see the possibility of Marxism again in the present global context, attending to the morphology of deconstructive practice is on the agenda.

FRAN   The final question then: "Would you like to talk briefly about the work you are currently involved in for your book *Master Discourse— Native Informant?*"

GAYATRI   The real answer to the question is no. (Laughter.)

FRAN   *Do* tell us your subtitle.

GAYATRI   Yes, a subtitle which I came upon about three days ago was "Deconstruction in the Service of Reading." Since there's so much unreadability in deconstruction, I thought that it might be useful to look at it when it is put into the service of reading. I'm engaged now in writing the last chapter of it, which is why I said I wouldn't like to talk about it. I'm just going to give you the chapter breakdown if I can find it and then make an end, O.K.? Again, I'm fudging a little—put it in your transcript and give me a chance, and I will edit it out when the moment comes. O.K., here is the chapter breakdown. The first chapter establishes the definition of the "other" of current radical criticism, of Third Worldist criticism as a site of desire. The second chapter takes three exemplary texts, (1) Kant's *Critique of Teleological Judgement*, (2) Hegel's discussion of symbolic art and (3) Marx's notion of the Asiatic mode of production, and looks at how a native informant might read these master discourses. The suggestion there is that in order to do Third Worldist criticism on a critique of imperialism, you don't just focus on texts that are talking about other places. The third chapter speaks of women's texts in the great tradition, and that's a reading of *Jane Eyre*, Jean Rhys's *Wide Sargasso Sea*, and *Frankenstein*. The fourth chapter is called "Limits of the Discipline," and that is a discussion of Foucault and Deleuze which I presented in Australia last year. The fifth chapter is called "The Other Woman I," and that's the young woman who killed herself in 1926. The sixth chapter is "The Other Woman II," and that is the Rani of Sirmur. The seventh chapter is "Looking Forward to Postmodernism," which deals with Rei Kawakubo, also a woman, and that is a talk I gave in Australia last year. This chapter ends with a critique of Jameson's essay on postmodernism. And the final chapter is obviously a conclusion which completes the book. And now writing chapter 2, wish me well, good bye. All the other chapters are written, by the way, so I kept chapter 2 for the end. I've written 2/3rds of chapter 2, so I feel very full of excitement. In fact now Fran is going home, and I'm moving upstairs to do a bit more Hegel. You needn't put this in the interview, but you may. I hope you're satisfied, we've had a good time.

10

Interview with
Radical Philosophy

In November 1988 Gayatri Spivak visited England to participate in the Radical Philosophy Conference, "Politics, Reason and Hope". An edited version of the interview between Peter Osborne, Jonathan Rée, and Gayatri Spivak appeared in Radical Philosophy 54 *(Spring 1990).*

RP   You have described yourself as a 'practical deconstructivist feminist Marxist'. What kind of relation do you see between these different aspects of your work?

SPIVAK   Marxism is the project of looking at how capital operates, whereas feminism has to do with theories of the subject—the development of men and women as subjects—as well as social practices dealing with definitions of sexual difference. This is not organised in as abstract and theoretical a way as Marxism. So it seems to me that the Marxist and feminist projects cannot be thought of as operating together, although they do relate. As for deconstruction: it is really the name of a way of doing these two things—or any kind of thing. It is much less substantive than these two projects. It is more of a way of looking than a programme for doing: a way of looking at the way we do things so that this way of looking becomes its doing.

RP   So you could be a deconstructive conservative?

SPIVAK   I believe so.

RP   Would you say that you began by learning the deconstructive approach and then went on to apply it in particular projects?

SPIVAK   I don't think so. One of the peculiar things about deconstruction (or the stuff Derrida writes) is that people who are taken by it will quite often say: 'That's what I was already thinking'. When I first read *Of Grammatology*, I felt I had understood what it was saying, and that it was a better way of describing what I was already trying to do. As to whether I was right or wrong, I've no idea.

For a time I felt ferociously angry with deconstruction because Derrida seemed not to be enough of a Marxist. He also seemed to be a sexist. But that's because I was wanting deconstruction to be what it isn't. I have realised its value by recognising its limits—by not asking it to do everything for me. I no longer feel that I've got to go out and bat for it in every field. I have very little patience with people who are so deeply into deconstruction that they have nothing else to think about. On the other hand, I believe that I am now much more deeply influenced by it than I was when I was so angry at it for not being everything.

RP   Your introduction to *Grammatology* established you as a person of full professional competence in philosophy and the history of philosophy, yet you repeatedly say that you're a literary critic, not a philosopher. What does this mean?

SPIVAK   It means that I take disciplinary boundaries very seriously. If you want to do interdisciplinary work, you have to admit that all those years of training in a discipline make a difference. You need to infiltrate the other disciplines. Graduate students in philosophy come to my classes and they say: 'I don't understand you'. What they mean is: 'You aren't meeting my conditions for intelligibility; therefore your work is not worth anything'. It's very hard from them, who have learned this worthless, dogmatic, door-shutting remark, and we should not underestimate the difficulties.

There is a great deal of 'nothing-but-ism' practiced on Derrida within philosophy in the United States: nothing but Heidegger, nothing but Hegel, nothing but the poor man's Nietzsche, nothing but mysticism, nothing but Wittgenstein even.

I don't say that I am *just* a literary critic. I say I *am* a literary critic.

RP   Many people think that left-wing theoretical activity in the United States lost its way some time in the last twenty years, that it ceased trying to reach a large public, so that it became an academic discipline of its own. What do you think of that analysis?

SPIVAK   Was it a question of the left losing its way, or the right knowing its way? Some people in Europe seem the think that the United States is the future of the intellectual enterprise, because the very heterogeneous tertiary education system there isolates a few elite institutions where these people can come and go, where there is a lot of radical chic. There is a practical political left in the United States, but it has no connection with the academic left.

There's also the question: in what kind of state does the intellectual have any real voice in the affairs of the state? In the newly de-colonised areas, the elite national bourgeoisie think of themselves as more political. They have a much stronger voice in the construction of national identity.

RP   You spoke earlier about the problem of deconstruction failing to meet certain people's conditions of intelligibility. Doesn't this cut it off from practical political activity?

SPIVAK I don't believe that I have a practical role to play in politics in America. Deconstruction is good in contact politics, not in broad planning. It's good for tactical situations . . . people one-on-one. In electoral politics it's not much use at all. It works much more strongly in the highly diversified politics of feminism and anti-racism.

RP Derrida has spoken of deconstruction in terms of the idea of 'responsibility towards the trace of the other'. Some people have sought a role here for deconstruction as a kind of critique. Yet Derrida insists that deconstruction is not a form of critique. What do you think of the attempts which have been made to understand deconstruction as a form of ideology-critique?

SPIVAK The problem with the idea of deconstruction as a form of ideology-critique is that deconstruction is not really interested in the exposure of error. At the beginning of *Grammatology*, it may look as if Derrida is a young hot-head exposing the error of Lévi-Strauss. But what he is really saying, contrary to Lévi-Strauss, is that the Nambikwara *also* had writing—because there are other ways of writing than ours. This is a bit like what Marx says about dissolving the mystery of money in the first chapter of *Capital:* that money is only a convenient way of measuring equivalences. We work with equivalences whenever we exchange anything. It's like Monsieur Jourdain speaking prose.

Derrida is interested in how truth is constructed rather than in exposing error. You could say that the text is addressed to the Nambikwara as much as to Lévi-Strauss. Deconstruction can only speak in the language of the thing it criticises. So as Derrida says, it falls prey to its own critique, *in a certain way.* That makes it very different from ideology-critique, even from auto-critique. The investment that deconstruction has to make in the thing being deconstructed is so great that it can't be made simply as the result of a decision that something must be deconstructed. It is a matter of looking at how one is speaking, knowing that one is probably not going to be able to speak in a very different way. If it is an auto-critique, then it is so in a much more complicated way.

If you want to get to the other side—as you sometimes must—then you must give up hope of doing it deconstructively. You cannot even *want* to deconstruct the person you want to ideology—critique. The only things one really deconstructs are things into which one is intimately mired. It speaks you. You speak it. One must not think that deconstruction is the only game in town. You can't say, as some real brief-holders for deconstruction would say, that it allows you to practice better. No, sometimes it stands in the way. But I'm not so sure that that's necessarily a bad thing.

RP In the Preface to *Grammatology*, you wrote of Derrida's use of the expression 'totality of an era'. Do you think that some conception of the 'history of metaphysics' as a whole is indispensible to defining the project of deconstruction?

SPIVAK Yes, I do. And it applies not just to deconstruction but to post-structuralists generally. They need a name for the general principle which seems to them to define things, though they keep changing the name. But it seems to me that 'the history of metaphysics' was a *bad* name. Derrida never really finished, or even undertook, that much-promised deconstruction. He hasn't been Son of Heidegger in that respect.

As for how deconstruction actually operates, it fixes on small things: margins, moments, etc. But something unifying is needed . . .

RP As a fiction?

SPIVAK As a necessary theoretical fiction which is a methodological presupposition. But the possibility of this fiction cannot be derived from some true account of things. If you take the theoretical formulation of deconstruction, you have a stalling at the beginning and a stalling at the end (*différance* at the beginning, and *aporia* at the end), so that you can neither *properly* begin nor *properly* end. Most of the people who are interested in deconstruction are interested in these two things. But I'm more interested in what happens in the middle; and I think the later Derrida is too.

RP When you spoke about humanism at the *Radical Philosophy* conference you seemed to suggest that difference might itself be thought as the unifying moment of a universal humanism . . .

SPIVAK People are similar not by virtue of being similar, but by virtue of producing a differential, or by virtue of thinking of themselves as other than a self-identical example of the species. It seems to me that the emancipatory project is more likely to succeed if one thinks of other people as being different; ultimately, perhaps absolutely different. On a very trivial level, people are different from the object of emancipatory benevolence.

RP Nonetheless, you accept that emancipatory projects require identity at some level, even if it is difference which must itself be taken as the name for this identity?

SPIVAK Yes . . .

RP Your warning about the necessity for some kind of identity here sounds very like Adorno's idea that totality must be 'both construed and denied' within a materialist dialectic. Doesn't this point to some kind of deep theoretical coherence between deconstruction and Marxism?

SPIVAK I don't want to agree with you. There isn't that coherence between deconstruction and Marxism—no way. The relationship between a reading of Marxism enhanced by deconstruction, in the broadest possible sense, and the extraordinary richness of the Marxian project is a much more interesting one than a mere coherence. There is a danger in making deconstruction coherent with Marxism. Everything that's useful in deconstruction will bite the dust, transformed into something that *seems* more radical. And everything that's expandable in Marxism in all kinds of different contexts will shrink into an extremely history-specific, race-specific, class-specific, trade-specific way of talking about doing things. A coherence between them would be worth no more than the satisfaction of coherence.

RP   How have you changed in the last twenty years?

SPIVAK   I ask less of deconstruction and I value it more. There is a real difference between my own agenda with deconstruction, and what most admirers of Derrida do with his stuff. I read Derrida much more as someone who is related to an extremely important arena of practice: the production of philosophical writing and teaching. Deconstruction teaches me that the politics of teaching we know in the academy is a *bad* politics—a politics of refuting, following your master, etc. It is more interesting to enter into texts so that the moments of bafflement can become useful.

The other thing that's happened is that although I'm against sexism I cannot think about women's solidarity *because* they are women. And although I find in Marx's analysis of capital the most powerful way of understanding what's going on in the world, I'm not particularly interested in privileging the class struggle. Similarly, in the case of the history of imperialism, I'm much more interested in the enabling violation of the post-colonial situation than in finding some sort of national identity untouched by the vicissitudes of history. It seems to me that that's the change that's taken place as—after twenty years of reading Derrida— some things have lasted in the wash.

11

Negotiating the Structures
of Violence

*The following interview was conducted on September
26, 1987, in Durham, N.C., where Gayatri Spivak
was participant at the Convergence in Crisis: Narratives of the History of Theory conference at the Duke
Center for Critical Theory, September 24-27, 1987.
The interview was secured for* Polygraph *by Richard
Dienst, Rosanne Kennedy, Joel Reed, Henry Schwarz,
and Rashmi Bhatnagar. A substantially edited version
of this interview was published in* Polygraph 2 *and*
3, Spring 1989.

POLYGRAPH   Of course feminism isn't identical with the Left, but you
mentioned that you were encouraged by Toril Moi's remark today that
a "materialist feminism" would perhaps set a more inclusive agenda for
the Left. Would this include an anti-racist position as well?

GAYATRI   No, I don't think so. I think these movements are very
discontinuous. It seems to me that each of these things brings the other
to crisis. And that's how it ought to be: serious crisis. In India one must
worry about the fact that women's labor is unorganized, as in many
Asian countries, but the project of labor organization is discontinuous
with the problem of feminism, because feminism can't keep itself occupied only with working class women. Feminism has many projects, just
as Marxism does in Third World countries. What Marxism really has to
offer is global systems. I think that the most powerful thing Marxism in
the Third World can offer is crisis theory. So Marxism is not so different
situationally. Feminism, however, is extremely heterogeneous, feminism
as opposed to the women's movement. Feminism is in fact willingly
involved with the transformation of consciousness.

P   One of the problems that Catherine McKinnon has is that she
neither marks the heterogeneity of feminism or Marxism, so we get a
totalized view of both. Radical feminism is becoming more central, but
is modifying itself to include more materialist analysis, and a whole
different thing is happening now.

G   In order to become really useful these things must lose their proper
names. The moment of the proper name is a transitional 'moment. I'm
not saying that women's studies as a discipline should die. Some women

say that there will come a time when we don't need women's studies, when all children will be born immediate feminists, as if saying that there will come a time when history should stop because everybody will know the correct amount about the past. I'm not saying that. But these things must bring each other to crisis all the time because that is the relationship between theory and practice.

P   Could you speak a little about what you mean by "bringing to crisis"? If I understood Jonathan Culler today, he said that the rhetoric of crisis marks our own provincialism.

G   What I mean by crisis is the moment at which you feel that your presuppositions of an enterprise are disproved by the enterprise itself. These are not necessarily moments of weakness. It seems to me that this is the only serious way in which crisis can become productive, when one feels, for example, that the women's movement challenges the project of feminism. On the other hand, one is not about to give up on feminism, but the relevant outcome, either from the women's movement point of view, or from the feminism point of view, is a problem and a moment when you must think about negotiating. I'm not saying that we live constantly in a state of crisis—crisis management is another name for life, right?—but it seems that if you look at even an old-fashioned revolution, there is a transitional moment; in the post-revolutionary moment, it seems as if revolution is no longer necessary, and that's when things start going wrong. As long as it's engaged in armed struggle, or as long as the enemy is present, things are fine, but after that things start going wrong because the element of crisis is absent. Anti-racism is yearly brought to crisis by anti-imperialism when we begin to see that even the most disenfranchised US black person can get a US passport, which is an incomparably superior thing to, say, an Indian passport.

Again, the idea in feminism that even the most disenfranchised man has more rights within patriarchal society than the most noble woman, this must seriously bring theories of class to crisis. You can't say like Zillah Eisenstein that "women are a class." No, but you don't give up the idea of class analysis either. That is the productive sense of crisis. Otherwise, living in a state of perpetual crisis is merely confessional.

P   Do you find the terminology of crisis appropriate to the conference this weekend? Is literary criticism or "cultural studies" in a crisis?

G   Well, there is a proliferation of these foundation-supported conferences and an incredible commodification of endowed chairs. And that is an alibi, it's not a crisis. Distinguished professors like Jameson, Barbara Smith, Stanley Fish, myself, we celebrate crisis. That's not a crisis, it's a crisis within quotation marks.

P But on the other hand we find the Left increasingly in retreat in the US. In the age of Reagan, we have to deal with people like William Bennett and Alan Bloom. There seems to be a generation which is lacking an oppositional position towards authority, and its direction is increasingly technical and profit-oriented, as opposed to "humanistic," value questioning. The crisis for theorists and educators is occurring in the public schools.

G I don't know as much about public education in the US as I should, but it isn't as if instruction in axiology is disappearing. That ideology is strongest which operates as nature. Axiological instruction is implicit in technological education. Look what's happening in old-fashioned economics. Do you think they don't tech values? I would like to see the business schools giving equal time to communism, which is an important economic system after all—as soon as they give equal time to to another way of approaching economic reality, I will give equal time to teaching capitalism in my class. I was walking about one night at the University of Texas, Austin, where they have a good large business school, and I happened to go past a classroom where a take-home exam was put on the blackboard. This was just before Grenada. There was a little exercise: "Suppose a communist country has just taken over a small island in such-and-such a place. What kind of modifications would you make in your development program in terms of project maximization and cost efficiency?" Capitalism, racism, and sexism are examples of correct theoretical practice. Axiology is getting taught in a much more implicit way.

P This explains all the articles we read in the Harvard Business Review about how to obliterate native cultures to maximize private industry.

G These cross-cultural impulses are very suspect. In these journals, even the relatively unsophisticated ones like the American Express Newsletter, people are saying that it helps the "developing" agency to learn something about the literature and culture of the place in which they are going to operate.

P A kind of neo-Orientalism.

G In fact what has happened is that now that the specific project of territorial imperialism has been dropped, since the middle of this century, and has changed into neo-colonialism, it is no longer necessary to cultivate a locally-resident community of cultured ideologues who will disseminate cultural imperialism. The interest in learning languages has subsided. The great Orientalists who really knew the languages, who were also colonial functionaries, are gone. This new emphasis is quite different from the seriousness of the cross-cultural enterprise that occurred during imperialism.

P Could you say it returns as pastiche?

G Yes.

P This raises the question of how to teach Third World studies at all. How could anyone learn a sufficient number of languages to study any generalized Third World culture? Just within East Africa, say, you would need x number of tribal languages. But to learn only one in depth could take many years, and one ends up only studying one specialized subject.

G Unfortunately, as you were saying, languages can only be acquired under the auspices of area studies. There are some in the US that are politicized. Not all of them—there is a solid history that takes its impetus from the civil rights movement, the black movement, several of these sites have become active in the US—but if you go outside of African and Latin American Studies, the politics are truly terrifying. You learn languages and then you begin to own your area in that peculiar imperialist-anthropological way. It would seem that if you learn one language you will become a "specialist" and this will bring your project of global benevolence to crisis, serious crisis. All that labor spent in learning a little-known language is in fact labor that can't be justified in terms of a global project. That is productive, because you will learn the limits of the damned thing.

P This raises the other question about heterogeneity and alliances, political practice, like that suggested by *Subaltern Studies** if that's a leap we can make . . . .

G You don't leap into the subaltern, you sink into the subaltern.

P Is that a category, the subaltern? How much can we put underneath this category?

G I like the word "subaltern" for one reason. It is truly situational. "Subaltern" began as a description of a certain rank in the military. The word was used under censorship by Gramsci: he called Marxism "monism," and was obliged to call the proletarian "subaltern." That word, used under duress, has been transformed into the description of everything that doesn't fall under a strict class analysis. I like that, because it has no theoretical rigor.

P In a certain way, it's like killing the proper name of Marxism as we discussed before—the traditional Marxist categories disappear when you begin to include the subaltern.

---

*Five volumes of Subaltern Studies: Writings on South Asian History and Society have been published under the editorship of Ranajit Guha (Delhi: Oxford University Press, 1982–87). For an account of this group, see Spivak, "Deconstructing Historiography" in Subaltern Studies 4, reprinted in In Other Worlds: Essays in Cultural Politics (New York: Methuen, 1987).

G   Yes, in some way, but Marxism is never far behind. One of the reasons I respect Ranajit Guha for doing Subaltern Studies is because he is not someone who has simply dismissed communism or the "Undivided Communist Party" (CP India) by not knowing anything about it; he has developed it into his position; he is not a non-Marxist but a post-Marxist.

P   Should this work be disseminated to a larger audience?

G   The actual explanatory mobilizing power of these signifiers—again the theme of crisis—comes hand in hand with the danger of their becoming out of bounds. In fact, if the word "subaltern" is appropriated by the US radical academy, the most opulent university system in the world, there will be danger. One has to be very vigilant and critical. The word "deconstruction," for example: it loses its aura of the original work of Derrida, but that isn't necessarily good, it brings with it a certain kind of danger. One can of course use the word "subaltern," but it is not necessarily good to reappropriate it. If one were to appropriate the notion of the subaltern to an American context, one must pay more attention to Gramsci and not focus on the work going on in India. One must recast Gramsci. Gramsci has now become an alibi for not being Marxist, just as Bakhtin has been taken up by the progressive bourgeoisie. Heteroglossia and dialogism are words that are used to cover over repressive dominance. Subalternity can become the same kind of dangerous signifier because it is not falling into any local space.

P   Your own reading of Subaltern Studies is critical, you read strongly against the grain of their texts. The insurgent consciousness that Guha tries to reconstruct from colonial historiography is not a text that can easily be deconstructed if one is to remain faithful to his politics. In other words, he seems to conceive of this consciousness as essential or solid, and your essay is an attempt to take that apart.

G   I'm glad you noticed that. I really read the Subalternists with that kind of love that I was talking about today, so that some of the opponents of Subaltern Studies in India think of me as a Subalternist; on the other hand the Subalternists realize what you are saying, that I don't endorse everything in their project.

This is still a route into, the proper insertion into, socialized capital, capital logic—the subaltern really had no access to those narratives of nationalism, those narratives of internationalism, nationalism, secularism, all of those things. So I think the implicit answer to your question was, given the active circuit of socialized capital, it is hard for us to think of a genuine subaltern in the First World. One can say the loneliness of the elderly subaltern in that situation, like the loneliness of the gendered subaltern and so on and so forth—but I think it would be difficult quickly to claim a subaltern in First World space.

P   In Guha's notion of the "prose of counter-insurgency," colonial historiography always in effect addresses its opposition or its negative movement, but latently—it is always reacting against that which it cannot represent per se. Is there a possibility of finding it here?

P   If this socialized capital movement means that we can't find a subaltern area in a First World space, has it always been that way? Was there once that space and there isn't anymore? Or, has there never been one because capital is always capital and it has its own marginal spaces that can't be subaltern? Or, finally, if capital is moving the way people like Jameson or Mandel say it is, will the subaltern be, or wherever the subaltern space is now, be eradicated or incorporated?

G   Not really, because capitalism has its crises—that's crisis theory—and the management of crisis takes place in the increased subalterniza-tion of the Other space. It seems to me that, if we are keeping with the analysis that Guha is giving of subalternity, it seems to me that what Marx calls the "freeing" of labor, that is to say, capital being explained without extra-economic coercion. If that is so, if that's the narrative of the self-determination of capital, [then] subalternity is not something that one would want to preserve. Capitalism, which in the areas where it works eradicates the possibility of there being subaltern insurgency, does not eradicate it in the world. Unlike Woodrow Wilson, who said, I believe, at some point that his dream was that everyone in the United States should become a captain of industry. Now that is patently impossi-ble under capitalism, because capitalism cannot survive without extrac-tion, appropriation and realization of surplus value. And this is even true under clean industry, because there is another place which makes this possible, the area of crisis management. When someone like Colin MacCabe says, when he was talking about "left solutions in the West," what he's actually not noticing is that the feasibility of old-Left solutions in areas outside of the West is directly tied to what he perceives as the non-feasibility of old-Left solutions in the West, so that from that point of view it seems to me that, if it is the spread of socialized capital maybe you can imagine a time when there will be no subalternity, but at that point, socialized capital will have sublated itself to socialism. You know what I'm saying?

P   Isn't this Baudrillard's point about socialism? You mentioned Bau-drillard's conception of hyperreality in your talk today. When reading Baudrillard one gets the sense that there is this notion of capital run amok—capital, in a sense, is homogenizing—socializing—all these un-equal developments which seem to occur in the Third World, and in a sense, colonizes the subaltern project before it gets off the ground. In fact, creates the notion of "subalternity" in a simulacrum so that it has a space to colonize. This is a very peculiar kind of thinking and not at all germane to the Marxist discourse, but we get the sense in his texts, and in some of the popular texts (like "Max Headroom" and other things) that this is in fact the logic of capital: a complete homogenization, and that opposing it almost does no good, and in fact contributes to the further incorporation-ability of capital.

G   If you oppose it within capital logic, yes. It seems to me that if you oppose it in terms of basically the labor movement now, in the United States, which is really a complete acceptance of capital logic,—collaboration of the upper reaches of labor and management—you know, if you oppose it that way, of course there is no possibility of anything. But it seems to me that the whole of a non-narrativisable subaltern insurgency is in fact the reason why it is called subaltern by people like Guha: it is not within capital logic that these oppositions occur. I think that their strength is that they're non-narrativisable.

P   The very paradoxical project there is that this subject then must be constructed.

G   But you see that points out—it becomes a paradigm case because the subject is in fact always constructed. But what I was saying this afternoon, that these so-called parasitical situations can become the model situations in some sense, they become the literal—they become the referent for theory even as the kind of theory I espouse knows that referents are constructed by discursive formations—so in fact what this stuff has to take into account is that paradoxically if what one hopes for as a solution comes to pass, the referential authority of the subaltern will disappear.

P   This is what you call 'paralogic.'

G   Well no, I was opposing myself to paralogy, as one finds it in Lyotard—Lyotard's notion of paralogy is a move that does not lead to an innovation, a move that does not lead to a telos—It's a powerful notion, but that notion can exist when, in fact, the paralogical person can oppose a master narrative. Again, it is in a certain sense, inside or outside. It is from within capital logic that one throws out that challenge. The real paralogist, funnily enough, is not someone who can be a self-conscious player in anything. See, the project of restoring, this consciousness-raising business, the project of making the moves self-conscious, which I don't see how a politics can avoid (and that is a crisis too) at the same time writes off the group. You make the subaltern the conscious subject of his—in the case of Subaltern Studies—own history. The subaltern disappears. So what?

P Gramsci makes that clear, too—

G Yes. That's what brings the—you cannot use the subaltern as an axiologically weighted term, like it's "good" to be a subaltern, like it's "good" to be working class, so let's talk about working-class culture—because in fact in regular class analysis, one works for the disappearance of the working class as working class.

P To get back to the American thing, if the work of the Subaltern Studies group implies some political practice in India—we'll beg that question, about what that might be—but based on what you just said about a non-narrativizable subject of opposition: can we find any link between that kind of thinking and American projects, like Jesse Jackson? Do you want to stretch any kind of homology there—

G Let me put it this way: the Subaltern Studies people are not perceived as political activists in any way. The established Left in India—and after all don't forget that the Communist party in India was Second International, they are not the Third—we're not talking about something recent. Remember that the "Undivided Party" has disappeared, I'm not talking about the current situation of the Left, I'm just saying that the Left tradition in India is an old one. They in fact find the Subalternists uninteresting, and in fact this business about the subalternists' notion of the subaltern not being true to Gramsci—I heard a scathing critique precisely to this point, in Paris: "Have you seen these people who are playing around with Western theories?" The reason why I like the Rainbow Coalition, to tell you the truth, is because it seems to me that Jesse Jackson is really making use of the circuits of socialized capital, and is a kind of "proto-Marxist on the ground." Because what he's talking about is gathering together the poor. It's not based on anything but the fact that there is an exploited group among all the subordinate groups. That, I think, under parliamentary democracy, such as it is, and electoral politics such as it is, that's—but that's not subalternity, that's in fact making use, transforming a condition of impossibility into a condition of possibility. Because under this kind of a system, all Marxist projects, serious political projects, turn either—quite happily it seems to me (I'm thinking of the old New American movement, which has now bitten the dust)—turn either to attending to local projects—very important it seems to me, or it turns into social democracy—almost approaching Christian democracy. And again, since we've been reading the Eighteenth Brumaire together—you know Marx has a wonderful analysis of the alliance between the urban proletariat and the petty bourgeoisie, producing social democracy, and although that analysis is now 130 years old, 135 years old, it has its point. So that it seems to me that in that context, I read Jesse Jackson's project, at least his avowed project, as something appropriately different from celebrating the subaltern. I think he is really trying, at least in the platform that he presents, he is really trying a kind of proto-Marxism on the soil.

P   You'd have to say he "loves" the Democratic party in the way you described—

G   You got it, and he will fall prey to his own critique, as deconstruction does. And that's not a negative mark, within the deconstructive morphology as I understand it, because who wins, loses. And on the other hand, one cannot not want to win, it is ridiculous to say that one doesn't. And one takes that into account as one forges one's practice. Therefore am I an admirer of Jesse Jackson, but not because I feel he is celebrating subalternity. Or pluralism. Well I can't vote of course, it's easy for me to say . . . Do you realize I've never voted? I left when I was nineteen, and in India one cannot vote by proxy.

P   I was interested in when you were talking about the graphematic structure—I was surprised, and the audience was surprised—you were re-centering the subject in Derrida. I think you said that when the Marxists work from Derrida, they take from him the notion of a subject that is decentered, and you re-center it. In my reading, and in a lot of people's reading, it is that much of Derrida's work is to decenter the subject. I was curious the way that was reversed, turned over.

G   I was not recentering the subject in Derrida. You see, deconstruction is not an exposure of error. As Derrida says, and now I am quoting, "Logocentrism is not a pathology," it is the thing that enables us—except, if because it enables us, we say that it is correct, it would be a mistake. That is all he is saying. So that, in fact, all that he looks at is the way in which the subject centers itself. He is not decentering the subject. The subject is—the subject must identify itself with its self-perceived intention. The fact that it must do so is not a description of what it is. That is the difference between decentered and centered. There is no way that a subject can be anything but centered. Logocentrism, phallocentrism, gynocentrism—all of these things enable. And deconstruction—the project starts with, as I say in the essay on "Breast-Giver",* with a misunderstanding of a rhetorical question. But the fact that the subject is centered begins with that kind of an un-endorsable error. That doesn't mean that the subject can be decentered. There is no such thing as the decentered subject. There is no such thing. If it is, it has already, that first "yes" is, the auto-position of the subject [. . .] the subject is, because it must give itself the gift of procreation, it is proper to itself. So to see, to read Derrida as if he is decentering the subject is in fact, it is a very possible misreading,

---

*In *In Other Worlds*, pp. 222–268.

and its is not a misreading. For he is describing the necessary centering of a subject in terms of a para-centrality that cannot *be* yet makes the centering of being possible.

We can't forget that it was in 1867 that both Fleurs du mal and Capital came in. So if Marxism is Capital One, Derrida is Fleurs du mal. If that's the division within which he falls, Derrida is decentering the subject. He's not decentering anything. He's just descriptive when he talks about the possibility of—and he could always be wrong. That's one of the things he says: that you have to take seriously the fact that you could always be wrong. It's not just a rhetorical gesture. Or, it if is a rhetorical gesture, you must take rhetorical gestures seriously. What he is looking at is the mechanics of how the subject centers itself. That's his critique. But that does not mean that there is something strange about Derrida saying, "I'm neither for nor against the Enlightenment, I'm neither for nor against feminism," it is possible so to make it useful, to read it as that particular statement of negotiation. Like "I am an anti-imperialist," right, one must—but on the other hand, I am someone who thinks that since it is the structures of cultural imperialism that has enabled me, I negotiate with it, rather than say, "Oh, let me decenter imperialism." In fact, Rashmi, in Delhi you asked me that question that day, and that was when for the first time I articulated the answer that feminism must negotiate with the structures of phallocentrism, because in fact that is what enables us. So it's not, I wasn't particularly recentering the decentered subject.

P   Let's go back to something earlier. Do you see women's studies as not negotiating with the structures of phallocentrism?

G   Yes.

P   OK, my question is really about the disjointed projects of feminism and women's studies. How do you place those projects in relation to phallocentrism? And negotiating?

G   I think both of them must negotiate, just as—but don't forget I also think phallocentrism must negotiate with feminism in certain ways, because what phallocentrism has done—

P   Does it though?

G   Of course it doesn't, I'm saying that it must—on the other hand, it does negotiate. Just as I was saying that the fact that confrontational humanist teaching seems to be disappearing, that it's giving itself alibis in such conferences and distinguished professorships, doesn't mean that axiological training has disappeared, as in technical education. In the same way, phallocentrism negotiates with feminism by foreclosing it—all negotiations are not positive—by declaring, when feminism is absolutely crucial to it today, that it is not so. It appropriates feminism—look at electoral politics, do you think the Reagan Administration could have come in on issues of "family" et cetera, if they were not negotiating with feminism? You know negotiation, as Derrida says, deconstruction opens the possibility of both the ethical and the non-ethical. If we think of negotiation only as a positive term, then I think we are sort of laundering it in some ways. Of course it negotiates with feminism, and it is our task to point that out. Now the reason why I am so strongly against feminism as table manners—you know, say "she" over "he," don't open doors for a woman if you're a man, don't light their cigarettes—not that these things are bad—but on the other hand, when this is simply superficial, that's identified with feminism and the phallocrats can be like real feminists. That's negotiation, isn't it? Geraldine Ferraro was a negotiation. To an extent, I'm not exculpating myself, I'm a negotiation. We're all sites of negotiation. On the other hand, as I said, negotiation in the general sense does not mean that one cannot point one's finger at the structure of negotiation in the restricted sense. The way I am negotiating is not exactly the same as someone else. So although the fact that a country has a female prime minister—as in Great Britain today—is not a mark of feminism, nevertheless one can point the finger at an Indian who claims, forgetting Sri Lanka, that India had the first female prime minister. It's not that.

P   Do you have any sense of the Italian autonomist movement, as being a positive Left-based coalition?

G   I think situationally it was very important. And I think the journal Zerowork certainly tried to relate the struggle of the Autonomists with Vietnam, and so forth, but I think that is always a mistake, with something that took a position outside of capital logic in terms of the Mirafiori riots, that it should not want to all of a sudden globalize itself. It was specific, it was powerful. I mean you've read Marie Antoinette Niccioc-chi's book called Après Marx, Avril?

In that book, where she identifies the subalterns, it sounds like the 1960s gone wild, and that it seems to me we come back to the question of where would you identify the subalterns. I think the proletarian is a theoretical fiction. It is a necessary methodological presupposition, the proletarian is that impossible person who has nothing but his or her body, all right? And it is absolutely necessary to assume him, it is absolutely dangerous to naturalize him, that in order to find the definition of a proletarian outside of employability is turned around. In order to found a model for a proletarian outside of the circuits of employability, as Marx says again and again, it's not—but then, claiming to be a member of that naturalized group is politically harmful.

P   In this case one can talk about employability, but we also have to talk about the reproduction of the employable class. It's under this notion of reproduction of the working class that the earlier categories break down. In the Wages for Housework group, for example, which spoke for the women at home, vacuuming the floors and procreating new workers, but technically unemployed—

G   That's right, as I said it's a situational solution, I have no objection to that. But when a situational solution is then theorized as a theoretical solution, then it seems to me there is a problem. Then there is a kind of canonizing of wage labor, which goes against the grain of our discussions of subalternity.

P   This is something about psychoanalysis in India, or in the Indian context. In a class recently, we were talking about psychoanalysis, and there are a couple of Chinese students, who said that the psychoanalytic model of the unconscious didn't really seem to translate into a Chinese context, and we were just generally questioning the cultural context of Freud and Lacan's model of subjectivity. Could you or Rashmi say something about that from an Indian perspective?

RASHMI   I really believe that I don't, as an Indian woman, have a model of subjectivity. While it seems to me that Professor Spivak is right in saying that sexuality has not been seen in the same kind of way, I'm not altogether sure what are the models available. It's a whole question that has been left out of the woman's movement.

It also meant that at certain point that these groups of radical feminists made very significant incursions into the political sphere, and extremely engaged materialist analyses of what was happening in the country. So for a lot of women in India it was a way of getting away from hegemonic control and I think that Indian male Marxists, in an absolutely pernicious way, the control on what feminists can say and the limitations on what they can do became so great that it became a space in which to have a different movement. You could have a magazine which talked about women with an incursion into mainstream politics. So that now many mainstream male Marxists are now recognizing the work that Manushi has done and the issues she has raised.

G   I disagree with you in one respect. When you talk about the Indian male Marxists as being of a pernicious variety, that sometimes is not explained. The established Left in India is against Subaltern Studies. So it is not so much a question of being male. At a certain point we become "genitalist essentialists." We also have to say that we are not talking about a country where Marxism is a luxurious claim of radicals. It is a place where there are seventeen electoral parties. It has three Left or Left coalition governments. What is more important for Marxism in Asia is crisis theory rather than trying to fit everything into the class struggle formation. And that's the problem with party-line Marxism in India to an extent, but as you said, the women's movement has not remained identified with the single issue, it has willy-nilly earned the respect of Marxists on the soil. Which is a very different thing from the dismissal of Marxism as male where there is in fact no viable Marxist tradition.

If one reads Political Affairs—it's the journal of the CP USA—in that journal what is said is: "We must bring in the blacks, we must bring in the gays, we must bring in the women": in other words, identify Marxism with the white male. I had this discussion with Stanley Aronowitz years ago when there was a very strange thing called the Marxist Union. They're not penicious—individuals should not be marked in that way. The are committed to the modes of production narrative . . . and so is Fred [Jameson]! That's a different thing from being pernicious. So when you say male Marxists are a pernicious variety it gets translated into all of those complaints about how awful the men were when we were on the New Left.

RASHMI   They have also been among the most receptive audience of the women's struggle, even if they have been opposed to it from the point of view of strategy, have been readers of the texts of the women's movement, and have been responsive to it. Would it be possible to say that feminism is at the point where it doesn't have its own theoreticians, it has been reactive, Althusser, deconstruction . . .

G   But why should it be autonomous, Rashmi? It is like finding the continuity of native tradition. I mean, I just don't know why we have to have a black theory and . . . during a recent interview, they kept asking, "Give me an example of an indigenous theory." . . . The only thing they could come up with was "Gandhian syncretism"—if that's not negotiating with the structures of cultural imperialism, my name is mud. Why on earth should we be on that impossible ahistorical quest for purist positions, that's about as non-materialist as could be. Isn't it autonomy that is suspect? Patriarchy negotiates with feminism, calls itself autonomous. Did you answer the question about the unconscious?

P   Well, that it was less relevant in the Indian context—

P   Wouldn't that be an indigenous theory of subjectivity?

G   When one thinks about the unconscious as the positing of radical alterity, the positing of an It in the I, doesn't matter if it's Chinese or from the Andaman islands . . . You see, the thing is when you say it's structured like a language, when it's structured like metaphor and metonymy, everything begins so go astray. On the other hand, Lacan after all in a piece . . . entitled "a Jacobson" . . . he said it wasn't structured like European languages, so that there are things that one can work with in the matter of alterity.

P   We were moving from the Freudian theoretical fiction of the primary persons into Lacan. Is the subject of the psychoanalytic model applicable worldwide, universally, or is it Eurocentric?

G   It depends on which model. The one applied is generally ego-psychoanalysis. V.S. Naipaul wrote that it wasn't applicable, and he thought it was a problem for the Indian sub-continent. Sudhir Kakar who is a very well-known psychoanalyst in India, has written an extremely well-intentioned neocolonial book about the Indian varieties of farther healing, it's like the savage mind, are just as wonderful as psychoanalysis. Except that I argue since it doesn't have the same institutional history, it's like recommending paralogy. . . . It's not something you ask about. Is it applicable? It has been applied. That's the epistemic violence I was talking about. . . . We work with the psychoanalytic. What's at issue is what has been the historical narrative of the institutionalization of this as the norm. When psychoanalysis loses its proper name and becomes pop-psych. So that people in fact diagnose what they're up to, make sense of their own lives, then I don't care what you say, in terms of native subjective theories, it is applicable. So that when Manushi analyzes patriarchal films, what she uses as a grid is pop-psych. So whatever you think of Freud and Lacan, that's what's applicable.

12

The New Historicism:
Political Commitment and
the Postmodern Critic

This interview between Harold Veeser and
Gayatri Spivak was first published in The
New Historicism, ed. Harold Veeser (New
York: Routledge, 1989).

In December, 1986, I sent some notes to Harold Veeser for my part in a forum on the topic above. In May, 1988, Veeser and I had a long telephone conversation, he in Kansas, I in California. What you read below is these two documents, edited lightly, as with this headnote. The substand of the topic announced above got worked out in between: the forum itself; my quick trip to France to hear French cultural workers—pro- and contra-Lacan psychoanalysts, Derrida, and a "deconstructive" psychoanalyst—debate Elisabeth Roudinesco's recently published *La bataille des cent ans: histoire de la psychanalyse en France* (Paris, Seuil, 1986), volume 2 (1925–1983), from the perspective of the intellectual-cultural politics of the last three decades in France; my eight months of teaching in New Delhi and Calcutta, involved in the politics of cultural identity as well as the culture of political identity as an unwilling visible post-structuralist marxist local girl from the outside; the uncovering of de Man's juvenilia; a long seminar on a thousand pages of Marx with a group of highly motivated students at Pittsburgh; a nerve-touching quarter at Stanford which taught me in a new and more detailed way, once again, deconstruction's marxist usefulness in the construction of the "third world" (the term recuperated for me as an Asian, from the Bandung Conference of 1955) (wo)man as object of study in the classroom—we are teachers, after all. Yet the two documents printed here seem not too different from each other. Perhaps I am making a virtue out of necessity, but it seems to me appropriate that this should be so. The immediate politics of human-scientific academic movements *are* in classrooms. The long term politics, from published and unpublished evidence, are constructed and judged by the future. The most ambitious hope of any academic would be that something like the gap I describe will stand, however obscurely, as "unpublished evidence." "Thought is . . . the blank part of the text, the necessarily indeterminate index of a future epoch of *differánce*" (Derrida, *Grammatology*, tr. Spivak, Baltimore: Hopkins, 1976, p. 93), a future that will bracket "our" thought, in "our" text, by interpreting it as that future is necessarily different from it, as that future necessarily defers it toward yet another bracketing future.

MLA Program Notes

I shall say what I always say: let us not make the immediate occasion transparent. "What are we doing here, now?" is an important question for deconstruction, so pervasive in Derrida that it's useless citing a particular passage. (The obvious problems with *saying* this are not unimportant but should perhaps be shelved on the present occasion. As far as deconstruction goes, this is the problem one has with saying anything.)

In order to come back to the question "What are we doing here, now?" I will stray into the following points:

1. We are not discussing actual political commitment but our fear that students and colleagues will think we are old-fashioned if we produce a coherent *discourse about* political commitment after the postwar critiques of Modernism and, indeed, of Sartrean humanism. (One way of avoiding this is to follow Habermas, but no one on the present panel is doing this.)

   Can one be necessarily involved in political activism by way of writing, and teaching deconstruction; or while occupying a critical position regarding Modernism and Modernization, is a different question and would be of little interest to the present occasion. The issue of "history" comes up in the larger political arena in a *situational* way and has little to do with the professed historicism of a school of literary criticism.

2. Because of this fear or unease, we tend to conflate post-modernism and post-structuralism. (Will cite Brice Wachterhauser's *Hermeneutics and Modern Philosophy* [Albany: SUNY Press, 1986], p. 50 and title "Hermeneutics and Post-Modernism" of the last section, to show extreme case.) This is a recent and *post hoc* phenomenon. This involves conflating

   Lyotard: macronarrative legitimation programs are defunct; hence "paralogy" (must be distinguished from "innovation . . . [m]orphogenesis [giving rise to new forms or moves], . . . not without rules, . . ., but . . . always locally determined" (Lyotard, *Post-modern Condition*, tr. Bennington and Massumi, Minnesota, 1984, p. 61). For examples of socialism/marxism legitimized by these postmodern pragmatics, see Ernesto Laclau and Chantal Mouffe, *Hegemony and Socialist Strategy: Towards a Radical Democratic Politics* (London: Verso, 1985) and Stephen A. Resnick and Richard D. Wolff, *Knowledge and Class: A Marxian Critique of Political Economy* (Chicago: Univ. of Chicago Press, 1987)

   Jameson: enthusiasm for Modernism is anachronistic; hence cognitive mapping for individual subject showing him his place and the place of cultural phenomena in geopolitics.

The Foucault of "What is An Author?" (both *The Archaeology of Knowledge* and the Foucault of the last interviews are here forgotten)

The tough semiological Barthes of the first phase (this involves ignoring the semioclastic and semiotropic Barthes).

This conflated mass is thrown into a vague old New Critical guise and we mourn the loss of history, the foregrounding of criticism and form, and the demoting of the author (often called the subject). This then leads into Derrida, who has, in a certain way, given New Criticism renewed life. (Though the adherents of the North Atlantic Way—whether new pragmatic [Rorty] or neo-new critical [Lentricchia] would object to this.) He is also taken to have written the narrative of the dead or decentered subject, said that history is bunk, and also said that everything is language. If time allows, I would like to show (by way of citations as well as commentary) that these are not positions necessarily implied or held by a deconstructive stance. For this position paper, it will be enough to risk the following rather hermetic statement:

> One argument about the subject in deconstruction runs this way. The subject is always centered. The critic is obliged to notice persistently that this centering is an "effect," shored up within indeterminate boundaries that can only be deciphered as determining. No politics can occupy itself with only this question. But when a political analysis or program forgets this it runs the risk of declaring ruptures in place of repetition—a risk that can congeal itself into varieties of fundamentalism.

> If I am asked to speak on Marxism in this context, I should be obliged to repeat a reading of certain passages in Marx that I offered at SAMLA. Not enough time has elapsed for me to have developed it any further. [The Pittsburgh seminar on Marx has changed this, but that work is brewing.] If there should be any interest in this, I might distinguish my position from Michael Ryan's in this respect, since recently both Barbara Foley and Terry Eagleton have spoken of our positions as identical.

3. In my judgment, then, 2 is produced by the fear and unease in 1. I will offer a few analytical remarks about item number 2.

   a. "Politics" here is allegorical for turf battles.

   b. "History" is a catachresis here, heavily charged with symbolic significance. [catachresis: "Improper use of words, application of a term to a thing which it does not properly denote, abuse or perversion of a trope or metaphor" (OED). My usage: a metaphor without an adequate literal referent, in the last instance a model for all metaphors, all names.]

    c. "New" historicism is a misnomer, basically in agreement with Fox-Genovese and La Capra here. "Old" idealism/materialism debate. If time offers, comments on Stephen Greenblatt, Jonathan Goldberg, Sande Cohen. [In the event, I only discussed Sande Cohen's *Historical Culture: On the Re-coding of An Academic Discipline* (Berkeley: Univ. of Calif. Press, 1986), pointing out that the political promises of its introduction, heavily indebted to Nietzsche's *Use and Abuse of History*, can necessarily not be performed in the impressive theoretical exposures in the body of the book. Is there a parable here?]
4. "What are we doing here, now?" A quick recap of deconstruction-bashing at the MLA, 1977–86. How it should and should not be done. In postmodernity "Knowledge is power" has shifted to information-command, and the pedagogy of the high humanities, or the appropriation of the popular into the pedagogic format of the h h's has become trivialized, or banalized. Within those sad limits, what the lowest common denominator of a specific politics of the humanists academy might be. For a "paralogy," with respect, is not feasible, or perhaps only too feasible. (There will no doubt be no time for a discussion of this last point.)

H.V.   How would you like to position yourself in relation to the new historicism?

G.S.   Whatever I might say about deconstruction versus the NH is a sort of echo without an origin, because my point of reference is the rather elaborately stage-managed conference held at the University of California at Irvine in May 1987, where I was not present. As I believe Derrida himself surmised at the conference, the conflict between New Historicism and deconstruction can now be narrowed down to a turf battle between Berkeley and Irvine, Berkeley and Los Angeles. I do not have much of a position vis-a-vis new historicism, because willy-nilly, I am not part of that turf battle. I think this is recognized by most people who more and more think of me as an anomaly. I am not a real Marxist literary critic. Fred Jameson does that. I'm not really a deconstructionist because I can't do those meticulous yet playful (literary criticism) or scholarly yet audacious (philosophy) readings. I don't get into the representative feminist collections. There are even wings that would say that I do not reflect the ways in which the critique of materialism should be done. That's an issue too close to me, I would start to gossip if I talked about that. At any rate, since I see the *new* historicism as a sort of academic media hype mounted against deconstruction, I find it hard to position myself in its regard.

H.V.   In fact your marginality has made you a particularly central figure. As you've said in another context, the challenge has been for you to shuttle between the margins and the center. How has your work empowered or suggested for years something that has begun to take place now? I mean the insertion of history in literary critical discourse.

G.S.   As for the question of marginality, you know, the essay "Explanations of Culture" which I wrote some years ago, was written very strongly under the influence of United States academic feminism which has been very enabling for me in order for me to be able to find a place. But it wasn't a place, like most places, where I could stay very long. And now I look at the concept-metaphor of margins in a slightly different way. More and more people have found in me a very convenient marginal, capital M, and this of course I have myself found politically very troubling. Thinking about that, I looked at the concept-metaphor of margins and began to realize that in the old days, marginalia were, in fact, rather important. Textual criticism in the pre-modern period is much interested in marginalia. In the early print culture in the West it was in the margins that the so-called argument of the paragraph or set of paragraphs was written. I would like to take away the current notion of marginality, which implicitly valorizes the center. It is, for the critic, a necessarily self-appointed position which is basically an accusing position. It seems to me that I would like to re-invent this kind of marginality which I now find: exclusion from various turfs. I would like to re-invent it as simply a critical moment rather than a de-centered moment, you know what I mean. That's the way I think of the margin—as not simply opposed to the center but as an accomplice of the center—because I find it very troubling that I should be defined as a marginal. I don't see how I could possibly have that definition except in terms of people's longing to find a marginal who is locatable. And as far as the business of real margins goes one of the things that I hear more and more these days is that Bengalis (I am a Bengali) really don't like what I do with Mahasweta Devi, whose fiction I translate from the Bengali. I am not particularly troubled by Bengalis not liking what I do. But a lesson can be drawn from it. Ngugi Wa Thiong'o, in his very important book *Writers In Politics*, has called an absolute demand upon the cultural worker: that he or she break her alliance with the native bourgeoisie. The authenticity of the margins, the defining of me as the spokesperson for "the third world," is undermined by the fact that my own class in India does not particularly like what I'm doing. I'm not representative of the margins in that sense either. Thus I am beginning to think of the concept-metaphor of margins more and more in terms of the history of margins: the place for the argument, the place for the critical moment, the place of interests for assertions rather than a shifting of the center as I suggested in that earlier essay. Now your question concerns the insertion of history into literary criticism. It seems to me that history, like most master words, is a word without an adequate literary reference. When people talk about history, that proper name is generally not opened up. Or if it is opened up, it begins to resemble something that in common parlance is not called history. If there is an insertion of what I do into history, it is very much into history as a catachresis, in the case of decolonized space the fact that what politically it would like to lay claim to—nationhood, citizenship, all of those things—that the actual supposedly literal history of those concepts was not written in those spaces. Culturally, of course, there is talk of ethnicity which is strongly endorsed by ministries of culture. But practically speaking what these spaces want is access to proper names, for which there is in fact no adequate literal reference, whatever you might call the narrative of reproduction. So if history entered into literary criticism for me, definitely it enters as catachresis, rather than as the real nitty-gritty about materiality, if you know what I mean.

H.V.   In the specific context of Mahasweta Devi's narrative (*In Other Worlds* Routledge, pp. 222–268) you have a section entitled "The Author's Own Reading: A Subject Position" in which she offers an allegorical reading of her own work as a story about British colonial oppression in India. You interestingly marginalize that author position as just one position among many. Does your response to Mahasweta, therefore, foreclose her own consciously intended narrative of emergence? And, if so, what advantages does your more complex reading of the same story offer to the subaltern to whom by your own scrupulous admission of interest you declare yourself to be allied?

G.S.   If Mahasweta is giving an allegorical reading which I find less than satisfactory, it is still not the reading which makes the mistake of thinking that the woman is India and her tormentors are the British. No. That is an *old* story. In fact, what she looks at is the structures of oppression within post-colonial space. The story has shifted under neo-colonialism in the greater Third World to an encounter with the indigenous elite, who are in fact caught up in the suppression of the subaltern. Then following through, Mahasweta's narrative of emergence, as you put it, of course revised in the way that I have revised it, is not in fact some kind of Indian production over against my production as a university scholar here. The point that I'm trying to make, and in fact I asked my friend, Henry Louis Gates to talk about the influence of F. R. Leavis on the formerly British African intelligentsia rather than simply of Africa as the tradition to which black Americans must look. Her production is also a colonial production, which takes shall we say a certain unwitting mixture of Leavis, A. C. Bradley, Raymond Williams, some amount of American New Criticism, perhaps all of this gathered together as the natural way of reading. Because we are after all talking about India as a place with a history, where the idea of literature and the reading of literature are also produced through the very mechanics that I am trying to critique. So it is not as if I am over against Mahasweta as the authentic voice and me as the U.S. scholarly reader. Mahasweta herself was a teacher of English so that what we're looking at is two different kinds of readerly production. One, old British colonial production transmogrified into an understanding as Indian. In her writing Mahasweta can question it; in her own production as reader, she acts it out. And quite another readerly production is critical of it.

The next item, where you say that I declare myself allied to the subaltern. I don't think that I declare myself to be allied to the subaltern. The subaltern is all that is not elite, but the trouble with those kinds of names is that if you have any kind of political interest you name it in the hope that the name will disappear. That's what class consciousness is in the interest of: the class disappearing. What politically we want to see is that the name would not be possible. So what I'm interested in is seeing ourselves as namers of the subaltern. If the subaltern can speak then, thank God, the subaltern is not a subaltern any more.

H.V. With some new historicists, the self-unmasking gesture can become a carpet under which to sweep complicities. In what way do you understand your own "scrupulous declaration of interest" to be a different sort of acknowledgment?

G.C. Most of the interest in deconstruction has been based upon the fact that at both ends of the deconstructive morphology there is a stalling, to borrow a word from Werner Hamacher. The stalling at the beginning is called *différance* and the stalling at the end is called aporia. This is a focus that one can discuss in terms of the institutional space in which the deconstruction program has been welcome.

Although I acknowledge the crucial important of these stallings at beginnings and ends, my interest is much more in the middle, which is where something like a practice emerges by way of a mistake. "Mistake" within quotes because the possibility of this mistake cannot be derived from something that is over against it, "correct." I believe that Derrida is interested in this as well. In an interview given to *Art Papers* some years ago, he has said that he's interested in the production of truths rather than exposure of errors. And to an extent that middle ground is the production of truth, which is an act of transgression, rather than an ignoring of deconstruction, as Richard Rorty would have it. Within that space, against what would you declare your own inability since there is no model where anyone is fully able to do anything. That's the declaration of interest as far as I am concerned, it is in fact a deeply theoretical move, as there is no room there for apologizing for the limits of one's own production.

H.V.   That's an important corrective at a moment when the New Historicists often seem painfully to straddle two positions: a will to the power to conduct what might be called a symptomatic reading of a Machereyan or Althusserian disclosure of what gets left out of a text and on the other side feelings of antifoundationalist guilt, causing them to disavow privileged insight and to acknowledge their own partiality and critical blindness, which disenables them; a paralyzing position to be put in. You seem to have pointed, with you conception of a middle between stalling, to a position that moves beyond stalled-out paralysis.

G.S.   At Stanford I was talking about crisis and about the enabling violation of the culture of imperialism. The students were there with me. They were looking at the words crisis and violation and integrating them into whatever it was that they were thinking of. In the last third of the course they began to see me just as they had wanted to see me right from the beginning, as a third world woman. Except by then I had changed the definition of that phrase and what I was telling them was that, if they were breaking away from ethnocentrism, they were wrong. Right? When I started talking about this at Stanford, they didn't realize it but they were actually in that crisis I was talking about. On the last day I told them, "Now I don't want to do counter transference, but look how the temperature has risen, because I've been telling you it's not so easy to construct us as an object of investigation. It hasn't been the usual kind of negative critique ('you can't know how to see our cultural systems'). I've criticized all arguments from ethnicity, all arguments from culturalism, and see now how I'm using post-structuralism and Marxism and using those tools and those which you think are contaminated. I'm telling you that your solution to enlarge the curriculum is in fact a continuation of the neocolonial production of knowledge although in practice I am with you, because on the other side are real racists. The fact that this battle should be won does not mean at all that winning it does not keep a Euroamerican centrism intact." That is the real sense of crisis, the real sense of what is involved, the production in the middle that *cannot* be endorsed by origin or end. There is no other way.

H.V.   Since you raise the question of pedagogy and crisis together, let me take that further. Minette Marcroft from a Marxist teaching collective at Syracuse University recently told me when she heard about this upcoming interview to ask you about the violence of your writing and teaching. That reminded me of your first words to me as we jogged along, "Are you a Marxist or what?" Is your pugnacious personal style a metonymy for learning to work in the crisis?

G.S.   I want to distinguish between two things here. First is my personal style which I am dissatisfied with. I would like to be able to write more sober prose.

Now that's a different problem, but if we keep that to one side I think the violence comes out of the conviction that the forces against which one is speaking are at their worst when they are most benevolent, and that they are most benevolent when embodied by the most vulnerable, that is to say, the students in class. The reason why I've been hedging the question of how do I put myself against the new historicism is that I'm profoundly uninterested in joining those battles with colleagues. This is something that goes on all over the world, wherever there are universities. But when one realizes that the real battleground is the classroom and the real focus is the benevolent young radical in the bosom of the neocolonial production of knowledge, and that one has to take away from them their conviction of where they are at their best without leaving them with nothing but a breast-beating, which is also something that is part of the neocolonial production of knowledge—"I'm only a white male," etc., and then business goes on as usual—that very uneasy predicament is I think what she is implying as the recognizable violence rather than the socratic method revamped, where anxiety is felt throughout the classroom, and you can congratulate yourself as doing correct politics. I think that's where the violence comes from. I've been fortunate over the past twenty-three years that students have been my best audience, that they have been able to see that this is a big problem—not exactly a guilt and shame trip.

H.V.   Stephen Greenblatt tells a story in his essay for this volume: when he was teaching a course called "Marxist Aesthetics" at Berkeley, a student shouted at him, denouncing his politics. This experience led Greenblatt to change the title and content of his course to "Cultural Poetics," which would presumably warn the Bolsheviks off. Is your teaching confrontational in ways that Greenblatt's would not be? Could one say that new historicists tend to resolve conflicts in texts and in their classes, whereas you tend to precipitate crises?

G.S.   The idea of shifting into cultural criticism for me is not a very happy response. That to me would not signify that I was moving away from confrontational to integrative. Look at Marx's texts. Especially the mature texts. They are all exhortative—to an implied reader. The division is between radical criticism of capitalism on one hand and cultural criticism on the other hand. And then comes a kind of complete trivialization of the category of class and this you see in the writings of many so-called post-Marxists. Instead of working *with* the notion of class and complicating and expanding it, it is simply rejected as an unexamined universalist notion. You know how in the 70s there were all kinds of contortions to avoid the word communist and so the use of euphemisms: are we going to call our group "radical"? What about the possibility of "socialist"? Now there has come another alibi word, which is "materialist." One is struck by the absence of any sense of what the history of materialism might be. The use of the adjective is an alibi for Marxism. I would not include Edward Said in this group but in that great critique of Said in his new book, Clifford does talk about what one can and cannot do with Foucault and one of the things that one cannot do with Foucault is turn him into a hermeneut who talks about nothing but the microphysics of power and thus make him an alibi for an alliance politics which takes for its own format the post-modern pragmatics of non-teleological and not necessarily innovative morphogenetics, giving rise to more and more moves. And it seems to me that the real story from this shift from let's say so-called Marxist interventions in literary criticism to a taking up of cultural criticism is not the story of simply a decision about one or another kind of criticism but it has a much broader social text within which it is embedded.

H.V.   You've pointed to the central difficulty of new historicism. You have said "I do not want to identify reality with the production of signs. Something else might be going on." That's an important caution that the new historicists have tended to overlook even as they pretend to negotiate it. That is, they move between this thing outside the production of signs by use of a metaphorics of their own. They refer to the traffic between these two levels as circulation. That has been the metaphor in a lot of the new historicists essays that I've received: circulation, exchange, negotiation. All of these terms are taken to describe the mediation between the cultural analysis of cultural artifacts and something else.

G.S.   What is that something else?

H.V.   That's never defined.

G.S.   Let me talk about Marx. It seems to me that the mode of production narrative in Marx is not a master narrative and the idea of class is not an inflexible idea. The mode of production narrative is a working hypothesis within the context. One should go to *Capital Volume 3* where he is talking about the law of the tendency of the rate of profit to fall and where he's talking about the counteractive process. There is a small but crucial section on foreign trade where he says that these specific analyses are no use in the area of foreign trade because these are places where the capitalist mode of exploitation has been exported without the capitalist mode of production, so if you really want to make calculations here you will have to go outside of the general equivalent—which is money—and look at value production in other ways, other codings, other inscriptions. We are literary critics. If we look at the production of Marx's own text, we see alternatives based on reading Marx's text carefully.

H.V.   In other words, you are not suggesting that Marx presents negative critique and no positive politics, but rather a limited field of alternatives.

G.S.   I am suggesting that Marx's texts are by no means univocal. The immense energy in transforming this to a univocal narrative has its own political history within our own lifetimes and one lifetime before us. You know this is not a very long story. So it seems to me that what is required of the people who would like to think that the choice between Marxism and micropolitics is the giving up of the master narrative—I think the real requirement there is to make time again to look at Marx. If one identifies Marxism with a master narrative one is conflating the history of Marxism with the texts of Marx, and the texts of Marx—I'm not a fundamentalist—the texts of Marx are precisely the place where there is no sure foundation to be found. In terms of decolonized space, if it is true that that's how Marx talks about how to analyze places where the capitalist mode of exploitation has been exported without the capitalist mode of production, then the idea that all their world literature is an allegory of nationalism becomes nonsense. Other ways of analysis can be enabled through Marx's incredible notion of that "slight, contentless thing"—Marx's way of describing value, a value that is not necessarily trapped in the circuit of the general equivalent in all possible contents.

H.V.   Is Catherine Gallagher not claiming the same sort of exemption for New Historicist cultural criticism, when she says that NH doesn't entail positive politics or political ignition? How does that claim differ from the claim you're making for Marx?

G.S.   That's a completely different question from global politics. So the first question has to do with what's happening in literary criticism, basically in the U.S.—its relationship to global politics is so complex. I mean what is it? Lit. Crit. next to global politics is a trivial discipline. Even if one were to look at the university system in the U.S.—we're not talking about the fight between Berkeley and Irvine—over who wins—but if we look at the four-year colleges, and the two-year colleges, and the community colleges and then relate to federal funding and Allan Bloom and the National Endowment for the Humanities, so on and so forth, there is very little resemblance to the relation between that and the third world and let's say the Monetary Fund and the World Bank, it's not even—the parallels are non-existent. Global politics is an arena in which the only way in which we can even begin to make some kind of a claim is that in the decolonized space, the indigenous bourgeoisie has a much stronger connection to the machineries that are going into state formation. In general these upwardly class-mobile people in the decolonized space go to universities which traditionally over the last 150 years have received ammunition from the metropolis, although often declaring that it doesn't do so. So perhaps the way we talk about the third world or feminism or this and that might become constructed as a simulacrum in those spaces so that the ministries of culture can be kept fed. Now that's a relationship which is not at all the kind of relationship that people who want to conflate the distinction between global politics with what is happening in the U.S. for baby boom critics would want to acknowledge because the fact is that they know very little about how systems of education operate in Japan, in some of the African states, in India, in Afghanistan, in Sri Lanka. These things are not comparable. If you wanted really to say there was any kind of relationship between global politics and this stuff, you would have to look at the system of education and the history of the university in those places. Otherwise, to think that that is an allegory of any kind of direct political action, I think it's the way most people who are in trivial positions like to imagine that they're in control.

I am always surprised by how these battles are inevitably always given the name of political forces operating globally. It's almost like a morality play. I always ask my students: "Do you really think that in order for the world to change, everybody must learn how cognitively to map the place of a hotel in Los Angeles on the geopolitical grid?" The claims made in the U.S. and how those claims are reprocessed by the Third World elite who then begin to masquerade as the representatives of the third world—it's the most bizarre narrative of its own.

H.V.   Touché. I suppose it's difficult to return to questions of literary criticism after that comment. But let me try anyway. At the *Marxism and Interpretation of Culture* colloquy a couple of years ago, you were teaching along with Stuart Hall. Stuart Hall's Althusserianism was a topic at that time. But whereas Hall took up things like Althusser's ideas about theoretical work and theoretical production, the new historicists have seemed to take up Althusser on ideology and the Machereyan variants for symptomatic readings devoted to locating the absences in literary texts, internal distances, things not said. You rarely do that sort of reading. What is wrong with that sort of symptomatic reading in your view, and what sort of readings do you do?

G.S.   Basically I learned first from de Man and then from Derrida the importance of reading absolutely literally. And of course the word "literally" is like the word "history." Like any master word, it is a catachretical word. I should say that, perhaps my early training at the University of Calcutta in the hands of a man called Sen gave me the first impulse in this direction and then the de Man of the '60's when I was his student, between '61 and '64 was certainly very interested in reading the logic of metaphors, absolutely literally. And then what I see of Derrida's reading especially of literary texts like Blanchot, etc., is a sort of inspired literalism. So I, in fact, do not go into a text thinking to diagnose the absences because you leave a lot outside the door when you enter as a doctor. And after all, a doctor cannot read the text as the body of her mother, his wife, or her husband, or their lovers. This relationship of love, which is the deconstructive relationship—you cannot deconstruct something which is not your own language. You know that passage I quote over and over again—the reason why in a certain way every deconstruction falls prey to its own critique is because the language that it uses is borrowed structurally and in every way from that position. Now in a sense the stance of the diagnostician is one in which, if it is consciously taken almost into the first step into the text, it is suspicious of love, of one's own bound place. Even if I know how to do it I would be afraid to do it. So I hang on to my literalist reading and then the reading that develops, develops. As in the classroom I am helpless, I'm never sure. But the symptomatic thing troubles me, and I'm not really capable of locating things. I would rather think of the text as my accomplice than my patient or my analysand. Unspoken stuff does come out, but if it comes out, it comes out against the grain of my reading. When it begins to clamor for my attention, it catches my eye.

H.V.   This makes me think of all the other people who have drawn on your work—Barbara Harlow and people at Texas, for example—have taken your work and moved in different directions with it. Would you comment on any of their projects or your feelings about having your work carried on in that way.

G.S.   You know, I don't think of Barbara as influenced by my work. I think of her very much as an ally. But I think the sources of her inspiration are probably much more Edward Said and her contacts with West Asian politics. I think she has carved out a theory of criticism which has found support from some of what I do but I don't think she's influenced by me. I think Chandra Mohanty is someone who's working in the same area. I think Lata Mani in Santa Cruz is. My work is not really on colonial discourse. It is very much more sort of the contemporary cultural politics of neocolonialism in the U.S.—And I think Lata's work is more on colonial discourse and she is a real historian. So there's a relationship there but not an influence. I have my student, Forest Pyle, who has written on the Romantic ideology of the imagination, which is about to be published by Stanford Press. Again, I think whatever influence I might have had on him—and obviously a dissertation director has some influence—he's turned into something quite different. And then

Jennifer Sharpe, who is my student, whose work is on the construction of the British university subject, again, her work is going in another direction. I have not formed disciples. That's a great thing. I am an autodidact and not a good scholar, and my teaching style is so odd that nobody in their right mind would want to imitate it—I am trying to get away from it. And therefore it protects me from actually having disciples. I feel that these people are allies. I have in no way exercised an independent influence on independent workers in the field, like Homi Bhabha, for instance. So I feel that Chandra Mohanty, Lata Mani, Mary Pratt, Barbara Harlow, all of these people, of course Edward Said as a sort of senior person in our midst, all of us sort of working in the same direction. In India I see connections with other people, some of whom are ahead of me, and some who have been working independently. But I don't see these people as really influenced by my work.

H.V.   Your teaching style prevents your having disciples or acolytes, perhaps, but I think also of the unusual cultural inscription of the people you name—Said growing up speaking several languages, attending the best Cairine prep schools, recreating himself at the old colonial Ghezira Club in the middle of the Nile, and you yourself, from Bengali aristocracy. Does that mean that people of the middle and lower middle classes growing up in whitebread families in the U.S. are somehow disenabled from doing this sort of work?

G.S.   No. One would have to be a complete cultural determinist in order to . . . how can I say that? No, I don't think that's true. We all transform our situations of lack into situations of excess. I mean that is the condition of impossibility, with parentheses put around "im." There are real differences between Edward and me, Barbara and me—all of us. Incidentally, my origins are solidly metropolitan middle class. How about those differences?

In fact, Said came to Pittsburgh to lecture with Romila Thapar, the other colleague I was mentioning, who is an archaeologist and a historian. She gave a brilliant talk, she totally obliterated the Aryanist argument in ancient Indian history. Said gave a talk on anthropology, and it was a wonderful talk. But at the end, some students asked about the people, and he was dismissive. I walked up to him and I said, "You really need to say this. After all, look at the two of us. We are post-colonials. We are in fact wild anthropologists." We, because of our class alliance, went out to do our field work—not only we but our parents did, not mine so much as his: my class status was lower—we went out to do field work in the West, not in the disciplinary sense, but pushed by class alliance and power lines, and we became successful, almost indistinguishable from them, unlike the disciplinary anthropologist. And we have now decided to look at the scandal of our production. So in fact, most post-colonials are not like us. Most post-colonials in fact are still quite interested either in proving that they are ethnic subjects and therefore the true marginals or that they are as good as the colonials. Barbara Harlow will tell you: she has very little in common in her early production with Edward and me. She wrote her dissertation with Eugenio Donato and then she went to Egypt because that is where she found a job and she really set about learning Arabic and so on because that's where she felt her work lay. There's nothing in her early production that would determine that she'd work there. We should not be cultural determinists. We live in a post-colonial neo-colonized world. And we should teach our students to find a toe-hold out of which they can become critical so that so-called cultural production—confessions to being a baby-boomer and therefore I'm a new historicist—that stuff is seen as simply a desire to do bio-graphy where actually the historical narrative is catachretical. If you think of the '60s, think of Czechoslovakia, not only Berkeley and France, or that the promises of devaluation didn't come true in some countries in Asia in '67. So one must not think of one's cultural production as some kind of literal determinant of what one can or cannot do.

H.V.   That brings to mind another area in which you have attacked cultural bio-determinism, that is within feminism. In the essay "Discourse and the Displacement of Woman," you say that the simple alterity of women is not a notion that is going to take women very far. Would you elaborate on that a bit?

G.S.   Anyone who can say "je est un autre," she's still strictly a "je." Look at the way this claim to otherness—I mean, it's becoming a scandal, I mean the damn thing is getting so institutionalized that everyone should wear T-shirts. This "je est un autre" reminds me of something else. Apparently in the book that David Morrell wrote after the filmscript of *Rambo III* there is an epigraph from Rimbaud's *A Season in Hell. Je est un autre*—"I am an Other" is also an epigraph from Rimbaud. As I was saying when you asked me, didn't I ally myself with the subaltern. I said by no means, I noticed myself as a namer of the subaltern. The subaltern is a name as "woman" in Derrida, or "power" in Foucault, and the name comes with an anxiety that if the political program gets anywhere the name will disappear. In that way I would say that women who claim alterity should see themselves—should in fact see themselves as naming rather than named. I think it's really bogus to legitimize the other side by claiming alterity. It doesn't move me at all. We've been reading from French feminism and part of the term of the class was how this kind of theory constructs third world feminism basically as an object of investigation for first world students. I was saying that reading against the grain doesn't just apply to our enemies but also to our friends so that if one reads someone like Irigaray within the history in France of the deployment of rhetoricity in a text, it becomes much more interesting than if read in this very old-fashioned way as declaring for woman's otherness. Most of the interesting people—feminists who have written about women's otherness—have also done a lot of other things, and the ones who are just repeating it as an incantation in order to justify their institutional privileges are dangerous. The dangerousness will not be noticed because they are precisely managing the crisis that the recognition of women's stratification would otherwise bring. It seems to me to be really rather obvious, no?

H.V. The question for a student of yours remains, how should one choose one's texts in the light of interests, desires, prejudgments of disempowered or marginalized groups? Ought one to choose one's texts on the basis of one's won interests, scrupulously declared, or should there be no conscious choosing of these kinds of texts at all?

G.S. It depends on who one is. If one were a student in a less than stellar institution, the ambit of one's choice is limited. If one is nontenured faculty in a less than stellar institution, one's ambit is also limited. I almost sometimes think that it is better to learn to read what one can read so well that one can be critical—rather than learn to read what one cannot hope to discern because there isn't an institution to support one's learning of languages, etc., and to read simply in order to say, "my conscience is clear." I was quite interested in Catherine Gallagher's use of Houston Baker's astute remark that those kids were really trying to free themselves of racism rather than help the black. Perhaps that's why I'm interested in not conflating that with what's going on in the general third world vis-à-vis institutions of learning. It's not supposed to clear one's own conscience—coming back to the Bloomsbury fraction—the social conscience in the end is supposed to protect the private consciousness. I don't think we should give it sanction as somehow adjudicating a freedom of choice.

H.V. What about the formal determination of those two essays, "Draupadi" and "Stanadayini?" These seem to be entirely unexpected, unscheduled formal achievements on your part. And yet that is the kind of claim you now hear Joel Fineman and some of the others making about new historicist work. Do you see your intervention in the form of the narrative as somehow related to theirs?

G.S. I don't really know if there is a relationship. I wrote the "Draupadi" piece in 1981 because I was absolutely shocked by the fact that I had become the spokeswoman for French feminism for *Yale French Studies* and *Critical Inquiry*. That was for me a moment of awakening. What the hell happened that I had become this? So I wrote "French Feminism in an International Frame" for *Yale French Studies* and I told *Critical Inquiry* that I was going to translate a piece of fiction—and it was interesting that it immediately changed to "on spec" rather than "commission" and so that was that. So in fact, all of the little paragraphs about deconstruction are there because Elizabeth Abel asked me, "How does all this relate to deconstruction?" And that's how that came about—by happenstance. "Breast Giver" was because I went to the Subaltern Studies Conference. They're all historians and they said that the paper should be based on something empirical. And I told them, look, I'm a literary critic: the only thing empirical for me would be a short story. What I produced was quite unlike the essay as you see it now. The essay as you see it now is a response to the indigenous Leftist bourgeois intellectual in Calcutta up in arms against what I seemed to have perpetrated. And so the audience there is very definitely that person. So if it looks like new historicism, well, I'm glad, though I wasn't trying.